The Presence Principle

This book is the first executive presence (EP) guide specifically designed for diverse professionals who want to lead authentically while embracing their full selves. It demystifies the often ambiguous concept of EP, offering a clear, actionable roadmap for professionals at every stage of their leadership journey. Whether you're navigating early career challenges or stepping into senior to C-Suite leadership positions, this book equips you with the tools to lead with confidence and grace.

What sets this book apart is its inclusive and visual approach to executive presence. Unlike traditional leadership guides, it addresses the needs of a diverse workforce and explains EP through accessible language and memorable illustrations. It also tackles modern leadership challenges—such as building presence in virtual environments and on social media—while incorporating expert insights from fields like artificial intelligence, personal branding, and visual communication. The structured "Inform, Equip, Empower" framework ensures each chapter delivers practical strategies, reflective exercises, and real-world applications. Written by an EP subject matter expert (SME) and a world-renowned opera singer who, together, have built and taught professionals around the world, this book takes the most empowering view of EP to provide readers with tools they can immediately apply.

This book is ideal for a wide range of readers from early-career professionals and business students to high-potential employees and seasoned executives. Sales professionals looking to enhance their influence and anyone seeking to elevate how others perceive their leadership will also find immense value. No matter your background or career stage, this guide empowers you to develop a strong, authentic EP in today's dynamic business landscape.

Alexa Chilcutt, PhD, is the faculty lead for Johns Hopkins Carey Business School's Executive Education Business Communication Certificate, and co-lead for the Academy for Women and Leadership. She is a certified executive coach who designs custom corporate training programs, and serves as executive education faculty for Texas Christian University's Neeley Business School and The University of Alabama's Culverhouse College of Business.

Carl DuPont, DMA, is an interdisciplinary artist, trainer, and leader. He is an associate professor at Johns Hopkins University who teaches voice at the Peabody Institute and Business Communications in the Carey Business School's Executive Education program. He leads the John F. Kennedy Center for the Performing Arts Washington National Institute and founded DuPont Consulting, LLC.

The Presence Principle

Embodying Executive Presence
to Lead with Impact

Alexa Chilcutt and Carl DuPont

Routledge
Taylor & Francis Group

NEW YORK AND LONDON

Designed cover image: Getty

First published 2026
by Routledge
605 Third Avenue, New York, NY 10158

and by Routledge
4 Park Square, Milton Park, Abingdon, Oxon, OX14 4RN

Routledge is an imprint of the Taylor & Francis Group, an informa business

© 2026 Alexa Chilcutt and Carl DuPont

For Product Safety Concerns and Information please contact our EU representative GPSR@taylorandfrancis.com. Taylor & Francis Verlag GmbH, Kaufingerstraße 24, 80331 München, Germany.

ISBN: 9781041037057 (hbk)
ISBN: 9781041021964 (pbk)
ISBN: 9781003624950 (ebk)

DOI: 10.4324/9781003624950

Typeset in Sabon
by KnowledgeWorks Global Ltd.

We wish to express our sincere appreciation to our families, who have supported us throughout the years and inspired us to be our best selves. Special thanks to the Executive Education team, our esteemed colleagues at Johns Hopkins Carey Business School. They have encouraged us in this endeavor, contributed in various ways, and their continuous help has brought this work to life.

Contents

About the Authors   *x*
Invitation   *xii*

SECTION I
Defining Executive Presence   **1**

1 What It Is, What It Isn't, and Why It Matters   3

   Inform—Why It Matters 3
   Equip—Skills or Behaviors That Enhance the Area
   *   in Focus 5*
   Activate—Try It on! 9

2 Initial Impressions   12

   Inform—Why It Matters 12
   Equip—Skills or Behaviors That Enhance the Area
   *   in Focus 13*
   Activate—Try It on! 17

3 Enduring Impressions   19

   Inform—Why It Matters 19
   Equip—Skills or Behaviors That Enhance the Area
   *   in Focus 20*
   Activate—Try It on! 24

SECTION II
Leading Authentically   27

4 Value Alignment and Leading Authentically   29

Inform—Why It Matters 29
Equip—Skills or Behaviors That Enhance the Area
   in Focus 31
Activate—Try It on! 36

5 Emotion Intelligence and Interpersonal Integrity   37

Inform—Why It Matters 37
Equip—Skills or Behaviors That Enhance the Area
   in Focus 42
Activate 45

6 Overcoming Limiting Beliefs   49

Inform—Why It Matters 49
Equip—Skills or Behaviors That Enhance the Area
   in Focus 53
Activate—Activities That Allow You to Try It on 57

SECTION III
Skills Building   67

7 Body Language and Virtual Communication   69

Inform—Why It Matters 69
Equip—Skills or Behaviors That Enhance the Area
   in Focus 70

8 Finding Your Voice   83

Inform—Why It Matters 83
Equip—Skills or Behaviors That Enhance the Area
   in Focus 87
Key Takeaways 92
Activate—Activities That Allow You to Try It on 93

9 Communicating Like a Leader   101

Inform—Why It Matters 101
Equip—Skills or Behaviors That Enhance the Area
    in Focus 102
Activate—Try It on! 111

10 Building for What's Next   119

Seeking an Executive Coach 119
Additional Resources 121
Overcoming Limiting Beliefs 123
Body Language 126
Effective Communication Skills for Leaders 128
Voice 130

Index   *134*

About the Authors

Dr. Alexa Chilcutt is a certified executive coach and faculty lead for the Business Communication Certificate program and co-lead for Academy for Women and Leadership at Johns Hopkins Carey Business School. Alexa is a subject matter expert in executive presence, public speaking, and team communication. Corporate clients have included Booz Allen Hamilton, Bloomberg Center for Public Innovation, Exelon Corporation, Hoya Corporation, Prometric, and German-based company igus. In 2024, Alexa contributed to articles in *Business Insider*, *Medium Authority Magazine*, *Forbes online*, and *Fox Digital News*. Her publications include *Engineered to Speak* by Wiley IEEE PCS and articles in *Workplace Health and Safety*, *MedEdPORTAL*, *Journal of American Dental Association* (JADA), and *Public Relations Journal*.

Dr. Carl DuPont guides professionals in reconnecting to their authentic voice through a transformative approach that bridges performance expertise with scientific precision. His work brings a rare interdisciplinary expertise to leadership development as an Associate Professor of Voice at the Peabody Institute, Executive Education faculty at Johns Hopkins University's Carey Business School, and artistic lead at the Kennedy Center. Carl's scholarly work has been published in the Oxford University Press and respected journals including *The Laryngoscope* and the *Voice and Speech Review.* Coaching clients range from Fortune 200 executives to international soloists at the Metropolitan Opera House and "The President's Own" US Marine Band. Carl has performed at some of the world's most prestigious venues including Carnegie Hall, the Kennedy Center, El Palacio de Bellas Artes, the Hong Kong Arts Festival, and Leipzig Opera House.

Invitation

We began teaching executive presence (EP) to high-potential midlevel leaders at a Fortune 200 company four years ago. The class was part of a year-long custom Innovative Leadership Program designed by Johns Hopkins Carey Business School's Executive Education program. Each time we taught the module, it was a transformational experience for the participants and for us as instructors. This led to the design of a three-day open-enrollment course for professionals from around the country and across industries. The class fills quickly and requires a waitlist when offered, and we continue to gain insight into why this topic resonates with current and aspiring leaders.

Along our own professional journeys, we have experienced successes and challenges. Success allowed us to grow in understanding what we were capable of, and challenges made us dig deep and sometimes pivot to discover an alternate route. As we teach and coach, we see executives and professionals experiencing those same moments. For some, it is about reinventing themselves in an authentic but elevated manner and for others it is about recognizing the power within and finding the confidence to tell the story of who they are and what they can do.

The goal of this book is the same as with the course, to equip and empower. This is done by sharing knowledge about the subject and helping you "try on" new skills. Readers are empowered to align their unique talents, values, and identities to the desired impressions they aim to create.

The focus of the book is on key characteristics of EP and providing actionable ways for readers to embody them. Section I provides an overview of what EP is and clarifies the characteristics that create perceptions of EP. Section II includes methods of examining and envisioning how to lead authentically and with integrity. Section III focuses on skill building that includes body language, voice, and communication. Finally, we have created a process of continued evolution and EP using The Presence Principle discussed in the *Build for What's Next* resources chapter. It is designed to provide a vision, values, voice framework based on the concepts discussed in this book, an iterative process of enacting the steps in continuous improvement and peak performance as an influential leader.

Each chapter has three sections:

1 Inform—Background information and relevance regarding aspects of EP
2 Equip—Mindsets, skills, and behaviors that enhance the area in focus
3 Activate—Activities that allow you to "try it on"

The outcomes of this book will allow you to:

- Gain clarity about what executive presence is and why it matters
- Understand the power of first impressions
- Enhance long-term impressions of values-in-action and expertise
- Identify your strengths and unique attributes
- Align your values to lead authentically
- Recognize the hallmarks of emotional intelligence and interpersonal integrity
- Overcome limiting beliefs, like impostor syndrome, and adopt techniques that boost self-confidence
- Enact dynamic and self-assured body language (both face-to-face and virtually)
- Find your authentic voice
- Communicate like a leader

You are already an expert in your professional arena. By virtue of picking up this book, you have shown interest in increasing self-confidence and expanding your sphere of influence. Bravo! Our book values an authentic and strengths-based approach to leadership development. We aim to give you the tools to dive into self-discovery and emerge as a leader who is more self-assured and influential.

In today's ever-evolving business environment, organizations are seeking leaders who not only deliver results but inspire trust, communicate with clarity, and lead with authenticity. Executive presence is no longer a "nice to have" trait—it's a strategic imperative for leadership development. Johns Hopkins Carey Business School's Executive Education programs, including both open-enrollment and custom corporate offerings, are designed to cultivate these critical capabilities.

This book captures the transformational essence of the Executive Presence course developed and led by Carl and Alexa, offering readers a powerful resource to grow as confident, credible, and compassionate

leaders. For companies and individuals committed to unlocking leadership potential at the highest level, this is an essential guide!
— Pam Williams, assistant dean Executive Education at the Johns Hopkins University Carey Business School

What participants are saying:

- *This course did a great job of providing information and insight on the mental and physical aspects of leadership presence. It was so valuable to allow us introspective moments while also taking us out of our comfort zones to be vocal and physical in how we present ourselves. Seeing the impact of our voices and how we project as well as learning tips on how to be more dynamic vocally was certainly a surprising aspect of this course that I valued immensely. Making us record ourselves, although difficult, really allowed us to see ourselves in an honest manner. Pairing us up beyond our table and across the room was a great way for us to break out of the comfort zones we created even in that space. Pairing with each other and then presenting ourselves actually made it a bit easier because you felt like you had an ally in the room. This course was very well thought out and flowed well.*
- *The exercises were great. They challenged us to go outside our comfort zone and permitted us to create and hone our messaging to maximize our executive presence.*
- *I like the practicality of the course. I also liked the factors that influenced EP were covered in the course, with practical solutions on how to improve these factors.*
- *The in-person class exercises we did—whether it was movement/improv with Carl or practicing our introductions and providing examples to Alexa—all helped us learn in the moment and forced us to experience the lesson in real time.*
- *The interactivity was key to the course's success. Both presenters were knowledgeable, enthusiastic, and engaging.*
- *We were made to do hard things, like present and be vulnerable in front of others. It was great, thorough and helped us to improve skills to communicate effectively and advocate for ourselves.*
- *The instructors and content were awesome! Day 1 was incredibly informative and valuable. I am SO proud to be a participant in the class. Not only do I know that I will be applying what I learned but I will be sharing (with) the newest member of my team. Skills and knowledge are priceless and, honestly, something often overlooked. I think the skills and knowledge will also help those of us that did not grow up in households where these skills were shared from manager/executive/ leader parent to child.*

- *I loved that there was a vocalist as a teacher to bring depth into the course!*
- *The course content was immediately applicable to my daily work.*
- *Steps of Impression Management were great to learn and digest as a professional. Identifying adjectives that we associate with and apply to establish our presence in the workplace was an eye-opener. Lastly, developing a pitch for self-advocacy lends itself well to our professional roles.*
- *Enthusiasm, warmth, expertise, collaboration, admirable.*
- *Always good to present 'real world' examples and practice-based experience! Very helpful to demonstrate the skills.*
- *I enjoyed the conversations around presenting yourself and engaging with those in leadership.*
- *It was terrifying and yet very effective to have to practice our self-advocacy pitch in front of the others in the course, and a moment of pure joy to see and support each person who did so.*

Figure 0.3 Image of Carl and Alexa engaging with Executive Presence course participants

Authors used AI tools as a research assistant. This included ideation, confirming sources, fact checking, and formatting citations.

Section I

Defining Executive Presence

Chapter 1

What It Is, What It Isn't, and Why It Matters

Inform—Why It Matters

Why is executive presence (EP) a crucial factor in your career development and success? A survey of 400 CEOs, corporate communication executives, and professional development managers, found 89% believed EP directly contributes to career advancement and 78% said that limited EP holds people back.[1]

Today, mid-to-senior-level leaders recognize the need to develop and display EP. A *Harvard Business Review* survey found 52% of men and 45% of women said being perceived as having EP is more important to being promoted than having specific qualifications.[2]

The problem lies in establishing a clear understanding of the factors that contribute to perceptions of EP. The Center for Talent Innovation found that feedback on EP is often contradictory and confusing, with 81% of those instructed to improve their executive presence were unclear as to how to act upon the feedback. This is why developing it is one of the top two reasons executives receive coaching.[3]

What is EP? It is a multifaceted concept, one that encompasses traits and skills that inspire confidence in leaders. Authors of the 2024 article "Executive Presence: Elevating Your Leadership and Career" explain that "At its core, presence is about the aura or the subtle-yet-impactful vibe a leader emits."[4] While it may seem like an ambiguous concept, there are concrete characteristics and meaningful ways to enhance EP through thoughtful training and development. No one is born with presence, but it can be demystified and developed.

In essence, EP is the quiet force that commands the room, not with noise, but with self-assurance, purpose, and a genuine regard for others.

DOI: 10.4324/9781003624950-2

Characteristics of Executive Presence

To get a feel for what professionals thought about the concept, we surveyed course participants asking them what EP meant to them. Here are some of their responses:

The ability to inspire confidence by one's mere presence.

The way a leader shows up or positions themselves as it relates to their actions, appearance, behaviors, and communication.

EP is the authentic, charismatic aura of leadership that surrounds a person who is dedicated to the service of the greater good.

EP is the physical and verbal way you communicate and display yourself in front of those who work for and with you. I think in the military they would have referred to it as your "command presence" which is essentially how you take charge and conduct yourself in front of others.

The ability to inspire confidence at all levels of an organization (subordinates, peers, senior leaders).

The ability to conduct yourself in a way that conveys professionalism, competence, and leadership.

To me, EP is about embodying professionalism and integrity in every interaction, communicating with clarity and confidence, and approaching challenges with a strategic mindset. It's the ability to lead by example, inspire trust, and drive impact through thoughtful decision-making and strong interpersonal skills.

EP is confidence in one's authority, credibility, and professionalism, while maintaining true authenticity and consideration.

All responses are correct, but the question around how we increase perceptions of EP or modify those that currently exist remains. At its core, EP is the ability to inspire confidence in your authentic leadership, expertise, and empowerment of others. Most articles or speakers discussing EP cover three general areas: (1) Gravitas, (2) communication, and (3) appearance. These characteristics alone create two conflicting ideas: (1) That you must be, or appear to be, an extrovert to convey a strong presence, and (2) that perceptions about our presence are primarily created during first impressions. Both notions are incorrect. Introverts, as well as extroverts, are able to display a high level of EP, and leaders continue to impact and influence others' perceptions of them over time.

More recent research reveals two main categories of characteristics: (1)Those formed through initial impressions or short-term exposure, and (2) those that allow others to recognize who we are as a leader based on our attitudes, actions, and behaviors over time. This provides meaningful insight.

The first category—initial impressions—includes elements like appearance, communication style, and confidence level that people assess within seconds of meeting us. While important for establishing credibility, these surface-level factors alone don't sustain leadership effectiveness.

The second category runs much deeper, encompassing the consistent patterns of behavior that reveal our authentic leadership character. This includes how we handle pressure, make decisions, interact with different stakeholders, and respond to both success and failure. These deeper characteristics take time to observe and evaluate, but they ultimately determine whether others see us as trustworthy, competent, and worthy of following.

Equip—Skills or Behaviors That Enhance the Area in Focus

Two studies create a more robust picture of EP. In "Understanding Executive Presence: Perspectives of Business Professionals" published in an American Psychological Association journal, researchers interviewed and surveyed 34 participants in professional development, executive search, and mid-to-senior-level leaders. Findings revealed ten characteristics. Half related to initial or short-term interactions and the other half were impressions made over time.[5]

The second study was conducted by Sylvia Ann Hewlett, founder of the Center for Talent Innovation. Hewlett surveyed corporate professionals from a variety of industries and revealed 11 characteristics that fell under the two broad categories of gravitas and communication traits. Her article titled, "The New Rules of Executive Presence" was published in *Harvard Business Review*.[6] Hewlett's research provides a comprehensive framework of the attitudes, behaviors, and actions that leaders need to project strong executive presence.

The characteristics identified in these two studies, presented below, reveal significant overlap in their findings.

Dagley and Gaskin's 2014 Study

Initial or Short-Term Impressions

- Status and reputation
- Projected confidence
- Appearance
- Communication ability
- Engagement skills

Evaluations Over Time or Long-Term Impressions

- Interpersonal integrity
- Values in action
- Intellect and expertise
- Outcome delivery ability
- Coercive power (negative attribute)

Center for Talent Innovation 2022 Study

Gravitas Traits

- Confidence
- Decisiveness
- Inclusiveness
- Respect for others
- Vision
- Integrity

Communication Traits

- Superior speaking skills
- Command of a room/Zoom meeting
- "Listen to learn" orientation
- Ability to read an audience
- Authenticity

As mentioned earlier, executive presence extends far beyond initial impressions of confidence, appearance, and gravitas. While strong first impressions matter, lasting leadership credibility comes from consistent behaviors that demonstrate character, authenticity, competence, and vision over time.

True executive presence encompasses a leader's ability to create buy-in, embody their values through action, and deliver results by inspiring others to act. It's built through the accumulated experience others have with your leadership—not just how you appear, but how you consistently show up.

Developing executive presence starts with understanding how others actually experience you. The critical question becomes: How can you ensure that others' perceptions of you reflect your authentic self and align with your genuine strengths, capabilities, and goals?

The Art of Impression Management

At the core of executive presence is the idea of impression management. It draws from Erving Goffman's impression management theory articulated in his book *The Presentation of Self in Everyday Life* (1956). Goffman viewed this through a theatrical lens and used this metaphor to explain how we manage our "front-stage" public image versus our "back-stage" private self, emphasizing the need to intentionally shape others' perceptions.

This theory aligns with Shakespeare's quote,

All the world's a stage, and all the men and women merely players: they have their exits and their entrances; and one man in his time plays many parts.

Our "exits and entrances" describe when we are away from or in front of our audiences. Front-stage describes the space where you are facing your audience. Here, you embody a particular role and attempt to connect with that audience to accomplish a specific goal. Back-stage is the space where you are free from an audience. Here, you are not concerned about displaying characteristics associated with successfully executing a specific role.

Think about various parts you play—at home as a partner or parent, socially with friends, and as a professional. While we are carrying the same personal values and sense of authenticity into each of these roles, the situations and audiences are unique. Depending on the situation, you may highlight different personal characteristics, behaviors, and communication patterns to accomplish a goal or to connect with others in a meaningful way.

The last part of the quote, "one man in his time plays many parts," reflects our personal and professional journey. As we mature and advance through a variety of professional roles, we are called to level up and adjust how we present ourselves and are perceived by others.

Moving from an individual contributor to a manager or leader is one example. You are not a different person, but in a leadership role you are called to accomplish work through others rather than by yourself. This takes some reinvention of you as a leader. It requires a shift in how other's perceive you. This shift in your role and responsibilities does not diminish or change your fundamental strengths, values, or interpersonal integrity.

Two questions to ask yourself: "What impressions am I currently making?" and "What impressions would I most desire to convey?"

Think of impression management as a tool to help develop your personal brand. In the 2023 *Harvard Business Review* article "A New Approach to Building Your Personal Brand," this is defined as "the amalgamation of the associations, beliefs, feelings, attitudes, and expectations that people collectively hold about you."[7]

Carla Harris, former vice chairman and managing director of Morgan Stanley and author of "Expect to Win," "Strategize to Win," and "Lead to Win," speaks about the importance that perceptions play in professional success. She states that "Perception is the co-pilot to reality" and that crafting and displaying impressions that are authentic to who we are while aligning with the organization's goals and values, are crucial to advancement and success. One strategic step is to determine the attributes associated with success for the role you are in or are seeking to fill.

Authenticity Is the Key

It is about identifying your core values, talents, and strengths while aligning them to the impressions that are important to you as a leader. Crafting perceptions or attempting to display characteristics that are not "you" work to your disadvantage. We may be able to create false impressions initially, but we cannot maintain them over time. You must also ask yourself, "How can I intentionally align my natural strengths, values, and goals with the impressions I make?" Chapter 4 delves more fully into identifying personal strengths and values and how to create alignment.

The three steps of Goffman's theory of impression management are: (1) Define, (2) create, and (3) maintain.

Step 1. Define the impressions you desire to create.
Step 2. Create those impressions through consistent attitudes, behaviors, and actions.
Step 3. Maintain impressions over time.

In workshops with professionals at all levels, this is our first exercise. It is a powerful place to begin. It is a "Reflection-Projection" activity that allows us to ask, "Where am I now?" and "Where do I want to be?" In the Activate section of this chapter, you can think strategically about implementing impression management theory by completing questions regarding Step 1: Define, Step 2: Create, and Step 3: Maintain. We will also provide variations of the questions posed to research participants in the 2014 study as a way to reflect on your own experiences with leaders and perceptions of executive presence.

Activate—Try It on!

Impression Management

Step 1: Define

Reflection

If I were to poll the people you work with, colleagues, clients, managers, direct reports, etc., and ask them to describe you, what three adjectives do you believe they would use?

1 Write three adjectives others would currently use to describe you.

1 _____

2 _____

3 _____

Projection

Now, think about your professional "best self." Maybe there is a position you aspire to, impressions you want to make as a leader, or a desire to enhance the impressions you currently make.

2 Write three adjectives you would most desire others to use when describing you.

1 _____

2 _____

3 _____

Step 2: Create

This involves deciding how to go about creating those impressions. Think about your presentation of self, behaviors, actions, attitudes, interactions, language, etc. Remember that only when your goals, values, and strengths are aligned authentically with the impressions will you be able to maintain them over time. List three tangible ways you can begin to create these impressions through your attitudes, actions, and communication practices (including how you describe yourself to others)?

1 _____

2 _____

3 _____

Step 3: Maintain

Describe what it looks like to maintain these impressions over time through consistent behavior. Are there "interrupters" or challenges to maintaining these impressions? A question to ask yourself is, "Is this a behavior I would naturally display in times of crisis or difficulty?"

Executive Presence

The following questions are based on those asked of participants in the 2014 research. Based on your own experiences with leaders who have made an impact, complete the prompts.

1 What characteristics come to mind when you think of someone who displays a high level of EP?
2 Describe someone who did not initially convey EP, but over time displayed a strong leadership presence. Maybe you became aware that people listened when they spoke, or this person was respected by others because of their actions, behaviors, or style of leadership.

    Answers to question 2 are generally an example of someone who displayed more of the long-term characteristics of EP. This is usually someone who came across as a quieter or unassuming individual that over time was valued because of their strengths and expertise.
3 Describe someone you've experienced that made a strong first impression, but over time their competence, integrity, or authenticity came into question.

    Answers to question 3 reflect an individual who knows how to make a positive first or initial impression but creates an incongruence between their stated values and talents as they interact with people over time. Think of someone you've interviewed who wowed you and everyone on a committee or board, but six months into their position, you were left asking yourself, "what was I thinking?" We have all been there, whether it was with a hire, leader, or colleague.
4 Is there a leader you would characterize as having a strong negative presence? Why? What behaviors did they engage in that caused others to be anxious or dread being in their presence?
5 In workshops, we find that many times the answer to question 3 turns into the answer to question 4. Negative behaviors continue to escalate over time and display themselves in negative ways that affect everyone they interact with, but especially those in horizontal or reporting relationships.

Notes

1 Sylvia Ann Hewlett, Lauren Leader-Chivée, Laura Sherbin, and Joanne Gordon with Fabiola Dieudonné. *Executive Presence*, (New York: Center for Talent Innovation. 2013).
2 Susan Bates, *ExPI Executive Presence Index*. (Boston: Bates Communications, 2018).
3 Susan Bates, *ExPI Executive Presence Index*. (Boston: Bates Communications, 2018).
4 Subrat Kumar Sundar Ray, "Executive Presence: Elevating Your Leadership and Career," *The ICFAI Journal of Soft Skills* 18, no. 1 (2024): 29–33.
5 Gavin R. Dagley and Cadeyrn J. Gaskin, "Understanding Executive Presence: Perspectives of Business Professionals," *Consulting Psychology Journal* 66, no. 3 (2014): 197–211, https://doi.org/10.1037/cpb0000011
6 Sylvia Ann Hewlett, *The New Rules of Executive Presence* (Boston: Harvard Business Review, 2024).
7 Jill Avery and Rachel Greenwald, *A New Approach to Building Your Personal Brand* (Boston: Harvard Business Review, 2023).

Chapter 2

Initial Impressions

Inform—Why It Matters

First impressions set the stage for perceived credibility, engagement, and self-confidence in initial interactions.

You may have heard that it takes 60 seconds to make a first impression, but most research suggests that first impressions occur within the first seven seconds. In just seven seconds, people assign value to your level of trustworthiness, competence, and likeability. While further impressions are refined through interactions over time, perceptions about executive presence begin to form as soon as initial contact occurs.

Snap judgments occur within "micro-moments." Psychologists Janine Willis and Alexander Todorov found that it only takes a tenth of a second to form an opinion.[1] They examined initial impressions based solely on facial expressions of a stranger. First impressions can be misleading, but are a key factor in threat evaluation, dating and friendship, and business opportunities. These quickly forming and automatic impressions affect our decision-making. For this reason, it is important to recognize the power of first impressions.

Think about meeting a leader for the first time or interviewing a potential candidate for a position. As soon as they enter the room, you begin to formulate ideas of the individual that shape the interaction. Why is this?

We are visual interpreters first. We notice the way someone walks or enters the room, stands, sits, dresses, makes eye contact, or even uses time as an indicator of ease or confidence. What do you display in an initial interaction? Are you aware of the messages you are sending as you enter a room or sit at a table? What visual and nonverbal behaviors are you engaging in? Are you smiling? Nodding? Making eye contact? Engaging with others? Are you potentially looking disinterested, nervous, or confused?

We are auditory interpreters second. When someone communicates in a clear, organized, and compelling manner, we credit them with a high level of subject-matter expertise. But it's not just what you say, it's how

DOI: 10.4324/9781003624950-3

you say it—your tone of voice, vocal variety (how you vary the pitch as you speak), volume, pauses, and even silence. How someone sounds, their use of voice, gives the listener a sense of the person's credibility, authenticity, and energy.

While first impressions are not the only impressions that matter, it is crucial to recognize their impact and the elements that drive them. Once we do, we can develop behaviors and skills that allow us to thrive in any situation. The goal is to feel more confident when meeting and engaging with others, especially in a new environment or situation. You are there for a reason.

Equip—Skills or Behaviors That Enhance the Area in Focus

Now let's analyze the key characteristics that drive first impressions and shape perceptions of executive presence.

Status and Reputation

This characteristic occurs prior to the initial interaction. Even before you arrive in person or virtually, others have formed opinions about you based on what they have heard from others, read, or seen on social media. Think of sitting in an audience waiting to hear a speech or presentation from a prestigious industry leader. If they are a CEO, chief financial officer, vice president of an organization, or a subject-matter expert in a specialized field, your expectations of their performance and presence are naturally elevated.

Preexposure attributes of titles and status, reputation, network, and past achievements all color how we perceive the individual's level of executive presence. If positive, these influences can create a "halo effect," granting the perception of executive presence prior to an initial meeting. It's assumed the individual will be self-assured, competent, and an effective communicator until proved otherwise. If negative perceptions are formed during preexposure (through social media, word-of-mouth, etc.), an individual is at an immediate disadvantage. Efforts will need to be made to counter those impressions through consistent positive behavior and proof of credibility within the field of expertise.

Appearance

Appearance is individualized. It is based on physical attributes, like height, grooming, facial display, clothing, etc. In terms of clothing or stylistic choices, there is no one *right* way to look or dress. It is more about being put together and "looking the part." It involves understanding the expectations of the role you are in, or seeking to fill, within the context of the organization's cultural norms.

Cultural norms vary. For example, high-level leaders in the technology field dress differently than high-level leaders within the financial industry. If you visited Apple in Silicon Valley, you would notice a more casual dress code throughout the levels of leadership. If you visited Morgan Stanley, you would notice a more formal style of dress and appearance. Regardless of the organization, you can display your own stylistic choices through color, cut, and clothing while operating within cultural expectations and the expectations of a particular role. In Chapter 7, you will find general considerations when thinking of elevating appearance and envisioning yourself at your best.

Confidence/Gravitas

We often think of confidence as charisma or an extroverted style of behavior. While confidence can be "owning the space", it can also be quiet. Confidence is seen as self-assurance, recognition of one's own abilities, or level of comfort. Gravitas can be defined as conveying dignity, substance, or weight. These two concepts go hand in hand. Together, the goal becomes to display a sense of self or self-confidence in your abilities, composure in the way you communicate, and poise or grace under fire. These characteristics involve both verbal and nonverbal cues.

Nonverbal (body language) cues include how you:

- Walk across a room or into a space
- Gesture
- Display or control facial expressions
- Sit
- Stand
- Make use of space
- Use time

Verbal cues include the use of:

- Direct language: "I recommend..." rather than "I think this could..."
- Active language: "I led the group..." rather than "The group conducted..."
- Minimal verbal fillers: Avoiding *uh, um, like, you know*
- Pausing before answering: Shows you are taking time to consider the question

- Pausing for emphasis: Working brief silences into speaking or presenting to highlight important information

In Chapter 7, we break down elements of body language and distinguish between insecure and confident cues. You will learn how to "own the space" and be yourself while exuding calm and confident behavior both in person and virtually. Chapter 8 begins with the anatomy of the voice and moves you through the process of recognizing the story of your voice to finally adopting methods that strengthen engagement and perceived power when utilizing vocal delivery of a message.

Communication Skills

This includes the ability to craft and deliver messages in a clear, concise, and influential manner. Whether communicating through email, via text, face-to-face, virtually, or through formal presentations, someone with a high level of executive presence secures an audience's attention and creates buy-in through articulate communication—effectively sharing your ideas and voice with others in a variety of situations.

We believe this characteristic is continuous, as communication occurs throughout the life span of a professional. Communication skills include both construction and delivery of a message. The ability to communicate with clarity and conviction is a hallmark of an effective leader.

Confident communication includes articulating messages that are:

- Organized
- Clear
- Concise
- Audience-centered
- Compelling

How you use your voice through tone, volume, pitch, articulation, and pausing for emphasis is considered an aspect of communication that adds meaning to your message.

In Chapter 9, you are provided with an overview of the goals and challenges of communication and given proven strategies to craft meaningful messages, whether delivering an email, text, project update, formal presentations, or engaging in a crucial conversation. In the Activate section of Chapter 9, there is a Communication Self-Assessment for you to complete to take stock of your strengths and weaknesses as they pertain to communication skills and you are provided with the template for crafting a Leadership Advocacy Pitch.

Social Skills/Ability to Engage

This characteristic involves the display of an eagerness to engage, sincerity, and friendliness. When you think about meeting people, socially or in business environments, your willingness to engage is an indicator of your interpersonal skills and self-confidence. Do you appear eager to meet and get to know someone by extending a hand, making eye contact, introducing yourself, starting small talk, or asking meaningful questions? Are you present in the moment with another, employing active listening skills that signify valuing the person and their ideas? Are you empathetic, putting yourself in the other's shoes and responding thoughtfully? Our ability to engage helps to foster trust and build relationships, especially in collaborative environments where these skills are necessary for problem-solving or goal accomplishment.

Takeaway

Looking at the five characteristics involved in initial impressions, what types of impressions do you believe you currently make? Taking a "fresh eyes" perspective, think of how others see or experience you during initial interactions. What are you communicating? What are you doing well and where could you improve?

A team returned from one of our retreats and decided to conduct their own "fresh-eyes" experiment. They wanted to assess the initial impressions they were creating for clients, so they simulated the complete client journey—driving into the parking lot, walking through the main entrance, and navigating to their office suite.

What they discovered was eye-opening. Because the team always parked behind the building and used the back entrance, they never noticed that the directional signage to their suite was missing. During a renovation two years earlier, workers had removed their door sign and simply never replaced it. Suddenly, the mystery of missed appointments and confused clients was solved.

This experience reinforced a fundamental truth: initial impressions matter—and we can't manage what we don't see from our clients' perspective.

Just like the team taking a different look at how people experienced them, it is also advantageous for us to examine the impressions we make during initial interactions. In the "Activate" section, you will walk through how others may be formulating opinions of you based on the characteristics discussed. Take a moment to complete the questions and create a plan of action.

Activate—Try It on!

Fresh Eyes Audit

Looking back at these five characteristics of initial impressions, which do you believe you currently display? Are there any of these five areas that you could enhance or develop?

1 **Status and reputation:** Prior to meeting someone in person, what is known about your status and reputation may add to or take away from your perceived executive presence. This includes current or previous positions, titles, achievements, social capital and network, and word of mouth.

   a What impressions about your status and reputation currently exist in the marketplace?
   b Make a list of artifacts (websites, social media, news, publications, etc.) that inform how people formulate perceptions about your achievements, network, and level of professionalism.
   c Are there ways to shift or strengthen these perceptions to ensure they are aligned with your desired impressions?

2 **Confidence/gravitas:** Confidence can be owning the space or quiet dignity. Degree of perceived ease, self-assurance, poise, grace, dignity, feeling comfortable taking up space.

   a Rate yourself on a scale of 1(extremely low)–10 (extremely high) on projected confidence. _____
   b What challenges, if any, do you have in projecting confidence?
   c Are there internal or external constraints to feeling confident within certain groups or spaces?

3 **Appearance:** Physical in nature, this involves presenting yourself in a way that aligns with your current role or the position you aspire to hold. Considerations include understanding your organization's culture, the visual expectations associated with specific roles, while integrating your personal style and what you feel confident and comfortable in.

   a Who is someone you admire that has great style while projecting themselves as a confident leader?
   b What aspects of your appearance do you feel good about?
   c What, if any, changes would you desire to make that would boost your level of comfort and confidence?

4 **Communication skills:** The ability to analyze your audience and craft clear and concise messages that resonate. The ability to share ideas effectively and utilize your voice. These skills apply to written and verbal communication.

   a In what ways are you an effective communicator?
   b What areas of communication present a challenge for you?

5 **Social Skills/Engagement:** The eagerness and apparent sincerity with which we meet and engage with others.

   a How comfortable are you with introducing yourself and starting conversations with new people in business settings?
   b What, if anything, holds you back?
   c What perceptions do you believe people have when initially interacting with you in terms of engagement?

Note

1 Janine Willis and Alexander Todorov. "First Impressions: Making up Your Mind after a 100-Ms Exposure to a Face," *Psychological Science* 17, no. 7 (2006): 592–598. https://doi.org/10.1111/j.1467-9280.2006.01750.x

Chapter 3

Enduring Impressions

Inform—Why It Matters

Enduring presence is about displaying consistent behavior. According to the 2023 Edelman Trust Barometer, 63% of professionals say they "need to see repeated performance over time" to trust someone.[1] A 2024 Gallup study found that a loss of faith in leadership and the ensuing disengagement of employees cost an estimated $8.8 trillion annually in lost productivity in the global economy.[2] Credibility, faith, and trust are not formed during short-term impressions, but through enduring impressions. "If you don't believe in the messenger, you won't believe the message."[3]

Executive presence that endures involves evidence of values-based behaviors and delivery of outcomes at the highest levels. It is easy to be wowed by someone in an initial meeting. Those first impressions, however, are seen as smoke and mirrors when one's attitudes, behaviors, and actions contradict their originally stated values, knowledge or expertise, and follow-through.

If you've hired someone based on their resume and positive performance in an interview only to regret it six months later, you understand. Maybe you've experienced being initially impressed with a leader only to form negative opinions of them over time due to the disconnect between the stated values and alleged expertise and the actual behaviors and outcomes. As you are seeking to elevate your executive presence, it is vital to take stock of what really matters to others in the long run.

"Positive leadership focuses on behaviors and interpersonal dynamics that increase followers' confidence and result in positive outcomes."[4] If we understand executive presence as one's ability to engage, align, and inspire, then positive impressions over time are crucial. This requires being intentional about enacting our values and interacting with integrity and consistency.

This requires a higher level of emotional intelligence. Self-awareness, regulation, empathy, social skills, and intrinsic motivation are necessary to bring our authentic and best selves forward. Enduring presence is not

DOI: 10.4324/9781003624950-4

a performance. It is based on an inner depth that guides our day-to-day decisions and interactions.

How do we move from performance to authentic presence? It begins with influence rooted in trust. When leaders consistently demonstrate trustworthiness, they build the loyalty, impact, and legacy that define true executive presence. This transformation happens through five key characteristics.

Equip—Skills or Behaviors That Enhance the Area in Focus

Evaluations over time occur through exposure to the individual. Looking back on the characteristics listed in Chapter 1 from the two pivotal studies, we have taken a blended approach to repetitive themes. These include interpersonal integrity (inclusiveness, respect for others, and a listen-to-learn orientation), values in action, intellect and expertise, vision, and peak performance (outcome delivery, follow through, and decisiveness).

Interpersonal Integrity

This characteristic describes someone who values authentic and enduring relationships. Leaders who show themselves to have interpersonal integrity acknowledge other's contributions, are inclusive, demonstrate respect for others, listen to learn, and display a human touch. People trust in the sincerity of interpersonal interactions and respect and admire a leader who invests in them as a person.

One action of investment is deep listening. Listening is often considered a passive communication skill. It is active and requires intentionality and presence. The goal is to remain in the moment and put aside internal thoughts and readied responses to fully invest in understanding what another is attempting to share and communicate. When people feel heard in a conversation, they credit the other with sincerity.

Once again, as mentioned in Chapter 2, there is a distinction between engagement skills and interpersonal integrity. An individual may make a strong initial impression regarding their social skills and willingness to engage, but over time may display behaviors that are insincere. A simple example would be forgetting details about the last conversation or that they met someone previously.

Values in Action

Values in action refers to the alignment of explicitly stated values (personal values or those regarding leadership, communication, team, or organization principles). If a leader states that they value "out of the box thinking" then one would expect them to be open to new ideas. An example of inconsistency between stated values and actions would be a leader who says they have an open-door policy, asking you to feel free to engage and bring them new ideas, while in practice they are unavailable and closed off.

Someone who displays values in action has, first, taken the time to identify their core values and understand how those values can relate to the organization or work at hand. Then, they are intentional about articulating their values and enacting them, even in times of difficulty. When describing this characteristic, professionals used terms like "genuine," "authentic," "speaks from the heart," "tough-minded," and "trustworthy."[5] In Chapter 4, we will examine ways to identify personal attributes and core values that inform how you define your unique value proposition and communicate what matters most.

Intellect and Expertise

Initial impressions of someone's level of intellect and expertise may be based on a resume, past achievements, positions, or accolades. Over time, we want to see that they are the go-to expert when information is needed or desired. Impressive intellect, a high degree of expertise or knowledge in certain areas, excellent judgment, and quiet wisdom all contribute to this characteristic.

Think of a time when you believed someone to be an authority in a certain area or to have a great degree of knowledge you could tap into or rely on when needed. If they prove themselves over time to be a reliable source of information, you credit them with executive presence in this area. If not, your trust in their subject matter expertise and leadership diminishes. The cautionary tale is not to overstate your depth of knowledge or expertise in an area if, in fact, it is limited. Just as we can build executive presence, we can also inadvertently undermine it.

Vision

> The most effective leaders don't simply respond to the moment—they architect the future.[6]
>
> (Brent Gleeson)

Vision is an ever-evolving process of recognizing the current state and identifying a desired future state. It has the power to be transformative as it brings people together to accomplish something larger than what currently exists. The process involves reflecting and envisioning, then strategizing, articulating, and executing.

Reflecting and envisioning are introspective steps. Reflection involves examining the current state and recognizing any gaps, desires, or goals. Envisioning is creative. It is the ability to envision a picture of a future desired state, what it looks like, feels like, and can accomplish.

The next step is to strategize and formulate a plan of action. A strategy includes asking, "What will it take, who is involved, what resources are needed, what is a logical order of actions?" Once a strategy is in place, an effective leader articulates the vision to stakeholders. "A leader's ability to paint a vivid picture of what success looks like and how it can be accomplished should unify their team around a common purpose." Clear communication around the goals, actions needed, people involved, and why the vision is important to stakeholders (not just the organization) is crucial to creating buy-in and reducing ambiguity. Chapter 9 provides a step-by-step process for how to create and deliver clear, concise, and compelling messages that aid in articulating your vision.

Finally, execution. Execution of a vision entails commitment to follow through, communication that is open and motivational, and SMART (specific, measurable, achievable, relevant, and timebound). A leader who can move a team from vision to execution is seen to have a high degree of executive presence. Once again, EP is seen as our ability to engage, align, and inspire – all necessary for goal accomplishment.

A survey conducted by McKinsey and Company found that 48% of executives ranked "presenting an inspiring vision" as the most important individual leadership behavior during a crisis.[7] When faced with large objectives and challenging situations, a leader who has vision and keeps it at the forefront is seen as proactive rather than reactive. A leader with vision can remain a constant source of guidance in times of crisis.

Peak Performance

Someone with a high level of executive presence is often, themselves, a top-tier performer. The concept of peak performance elevates the previously cited characteristics of outcome delivery, follow-through, and decision-making skills. While those three characteristics are important to getting work done, there is a need to think "next level."

As an individual contributor, you are solely responsible for delivering outcomes based on personal work. As a leader, you are getting a larger scope of work accomplished through a collective. Whether as an individual contributor or leader, excellence in the quality and execution of work is a hallmark of executive presence. Peak performers are seen as energetic, hard-working professionals who deliver exceptional results while inspiring and enabling others to do the same.

Traits of peak performers include:

- Emotionally intelligent
- Accountable
- Visionary
- Action-oriented
- Consistent
- In control of time
- Focused
- High-performance mindset
- Decisive
- Influential
- Adaptable
- Life-long learner
- Other-centric

Authentic leaders do not copy other's behaviors while interacting and learning, but act based on their internal values. Identify the characteristics from above that you excel in and lean into those areas as hallmarks of your leadership.

Pro Tip: It is not about getting the *most* done. Quantity over quality can "scatter your force" as Ralph Waldo Emerson notes in "Self-Reliance."[8] It is about choosing wisely what to focus on and where to expend precious energy. Choose work that has a larger return on investment and that aligns with your overarching goals.

Negative Presence

In Chapter 1, you reflected on a leader whose powerful presence created anxiety or negativity in others. This phenomenon has a name: Coercive Power Use. Research reveals this dark side of executive presence - leaders who generate influence through fear and discomfort rather than genuine authority.

Leaders who are coercive cause people to feel threatened and vulnerable, diminished and unvalued, and ultimately keep them off balance. This is a non-trusting relationship. Individuals who display coercive power use might engage in destructive behaviors that include micromanaging to the extreme, delivering negative feedback in destructive ways or via "public whippings," meaning reprimands in front of others, and may use intimidation and fear-inducing tactics to get their way.

Popular culture examples of this type of leader include Miranda Priestly from *The Devil Wears Prada*, Terence Fletcher from *Whiplash*, Raymond Tusk from *House of Cards*, or Gordon Gekko in *Wall Street*.

The Takeaway

The five characteristics associated with evaluations over time should paint a clearer picture of what executive presence is and how impressions are formed and maintained. In the following chapters we begin to focus on the inner work and then skills necessary to give you the confidence to realize your "best self". Chapter 4 walks you through the process of identifying your positive attributes and values and provides strategies to communicate and convey them. Chapter 5 ties our understanding of EQ (emotional intelligence) to our ability to engage in authentic interactions. Chapter 6 demystifies the common challenge of impostor syndrome and gives you tools taken from sports and performance psychology to keep our negative inner voice at bay and learn how to embrace our best selves. Chapter 7 empowers you with tools to understand and navigate nonverbal communication including body language in both in-person and virtual environments. Chapter 8 focuses on the power of your unique voice, both physiologically and metaphorically. What does it mean to have a voice? What stories have you been told about your voice? There is power in finding and using your voice! Chapter 9 equips you with clear strategies for communicating. You will learn ways to cut through the noise and be seen as an impactful and influential communicator and leader. Chapter 10 provides you with resources to "Build for What's Next" that include avenues for continued professional development and learning. It will be an adventure!

Activate—Try It on!

Enduring Impressions Audit

On a scale from 0 to 7, rate yourself according to what you believe others currently perceive.

0 - Negative perceptions — 3 - Neutral Perceptions —

7 - Outstanding Perceptions

Looking back at these five characteristics developed over time and long-term exposure, take time to answer the following questions:

1 **Interpersonal integrity:** Leaders who show themselves to have interpersonal integrity acknowledge others' contributions, are inclusive, demonstrate respect for others, listen to learn, and display a human touch.

    0   2   3   4   5   6   7

2 **Values in action:** This refers to the alignment of stated values (personal values or those regarding leadership, communication, team, or organization principles) to actions in various situations over time.

    0   2   3   4   5   6   7

3 **Intellect and expertise:** An impressive intellect, a high degree of expertise or knowledge in certain areas, excellent judgment, and quiet wisdom.

    0   2   3   4   5   6   7

4 **Vision:** The ever-evolving process of recognizing the current state and identifying a desired future state. Vision is determined through a process of reflection and envisioning, and then strategizing, articulating, and executing.

    0   2   3   4   5   6   7

5 **Peak performance:** Delivery of high-quality work, whether as an individual contributor or leader.

    0   2   3   4   5   6   7

6 What were the characteristics you rated yourself at 5-7?
7 What communication or behaviors are you employing that currently enhance or confirm these characteristics?
8 What were the characteristics you rated yourself 0-4?
9 What challenges do you face with these characteristics, and what might you do to strengthen them?

Notes

1 Edelman. 2023. *Edelman Trust Barometer 2023.* https://www.edelman.com/trust

2 "Employee Engagement: 10 Best Practices for Improving Your Culture." *CIO*, 2023.

3 James M. Kouzes and Barry Z. Posner, *The Leadership Challenge: How to Make Extraordinary Things Happen in Organizations* (Hoboken, NJ: Wiley, 2017).

4 Julia E. Hoch, William H. Bommer, James H. Dulebohn, and Dongyuan Wu, "Do Ethical, Authentic, and Servant Leadership Explain Variance above and beyond Transformational Leadership? A Meta-Analysis," *Journal of Management* 44, no. 2 (2018): 501–529, https://doi.org/10.1177/0149206316665461

5 Gavin R. Dagley and Cadeyrn J. Gaskin, "Understanding Executive Presence: Perspectives of Business Professionals," *Consulting Psychology Journal* 66, no. 3 (2014): 197–211, https://doi.org/10.1037/cpb0000011

6 Brent Gleeson, "How Bold Leadership Vision Drives Growth and Talent-Driven Cultures," *Forbes*, May 13, 2025. https://www.forbes.com/sites/brentgleeson/2025/05/13/how-bold-leadership-vision-drives-growth-and-talent-driven-cultures/

7 *Leading Off*, McKinsey & Company, March 14, 2022, https://www.mckinsey.com/~/media/mckinsey/email/leadingoff/2022/03/14/2022-03-14b.html

8 Ralph Waldo Emerson, "Self-Reliance," in *Essays and Lectures*, ed. Joel Porte (New York: Library of America, 1983), 259–282.

Section II

Leading Authentically

Chapter 4

Value Alignment and Leading Authentically

Inform—Why It Matters

Values in action were identified by 97% of surveyed professionals as a key attribute of executive presence, described as "the extent to which the person acts in accordance with principled personal values."[1] Hewlett's 2022 survey results similarly emphasized "authenticity" and "integrity" as central components.[2] Participants used additional descriptors including genuine, courageous, authentic with follow-through, and trustworthy—qualities that collectively enable leaders to earn deep respect and maintain enduring presence.[3]

Today, we choose to follow a genuine, values-based leader we trust, one who shows us who they are by clearly stating their values and demonstrating them through consistent behavior over time. When a leader's behaviors are incongruent with their stated values or they are seen to be inauthentic, trust erodes.

You do not need to be in an executive-level position to begin creating perceptions about your core values and unique leadership attributes. In fact, the sooner you identify what matters most and how to convey it, the sooner people will take note of your leadership potential. Hewlett states that, "Nowadays, to be seen as leadership material, executives are expected to reveal who they fundamentally are—not mimic some dated, idealized model."[4]

> A person is authentic if they maintain this balance in the process of realizing their own values and needs, their individuality and uniqueness, while at the same time living together with others and the world, meeting the needs and challenges of these relationships in interdependence and solidarity.[5]

Defining who we are fundamentally is not a new concept. In ancient Greece, the saying 'Know thyself" was inscribed in the Temple of Apollo

DOI: 10.4324/9781003624950-6

at Delphi. The power associated with this phrase has a direct meaning for today's idea of executive presence. The Greek idea of to "know thyself" is "to have full power," whereby one is the master of their own domain. When we authentically express our strengths, vision, values, and personality as leaders, we create an openness that naturally draws others to us.

As we examine the idea of authentic leadership, below are a few definitions taken from literature on the subject and highlighted in, "Leading Change Authentically: How Leaders Influence Follower Responses to Complex Change."[6] In these statements, authenticity and values are interdependent. Which definition(s) resonate with you?

- Authentic leaders do not copy others' behaviors while interacting and learning from others, but act based on their internal values.
- Authenticity is the extent to which an individual is true to oneself by emphasizing core values and acts accordingly.
- One is authentic if one maintains a balance in the process of realizing one's own values and needs and one's individuality and uniqueness, while at the same time living together with others and the world, meeting the needs and challenges of these relationships in interdependence and solidarity.
- An authentic leader knows himself or herself in terms of thoughts and emotions and develops transparent relationships with followers. In addition, an authentic leader has a considerable awareness of their personal judgments and biases that enable them to have control of their thoughts and emotions.

What are your current thoughts on the following questions?

How do you currently convey authenticity?
What does it mean to develop a professional persona grounded in integrity?
How can you align your true strengths and values with attitudes, actions, and communication?

Authenticity, as it relates to leadership and executive presence, consists of four elements:

1 Self-understanding
2 Unbiased processing of personal strengths and weaknesses
3 Values in action (acting on guiding principles rather than external validation or reward)
4 Interpersonal integrity

Equip—Skills or Behaviors That Enhance the Area in Focus

Identifying Your Strengths-Based Attributes

Many times, we are intuitively aware of our strengths but do not recognize how they make us a unique contributor. Completing this activity will allow you to take ownership of the qualities that come naturally to you or areas in which you excel. It is also a tool that helps combat impostor syndrome, as discussed in detail in Chapter 6. Part of impostor syndrome comes from not recognizing your unique strengths and how they contribute to your success, along with adopting the notion that what is easy for you must be easy for others. This is a limiting belief, one that can be overcome through auditing the talents and attributes that contribute to your success.

The goal is not to be all things to all people in all situations. You can't excel at every facet of business. Some of us are doers, some are relaters, influencers, or thinkers. The art of leadership is to embrace your strengths and then empower others by recognizing theirs. Together, this strengths-based approach contributes to productive collaboration and goal accomplishment.

Here is a list of attributes that facilitates thinking about what you bring to the table. Take a moment to circle the qualities or attributes that resonate with you. Finish the sentence, "I am a…"

Teacher	Thinker	Storyteller
Adviser	Planner	Persuader
Mentor	Organizer	Pragmatist
Mediator	Executor	Coordinator
Collaborator	Crisis manager	Driver
Listener	Communicator	Visionary
Connector	Enthusiast	Risk-taker
Strategic thinker	Cheerleader	Innovator
Decision-maker	Optimist	Futurist
Problem-solver	Relationship builder	Creative
Team builder	Influencer	

In Chapter 1 you were asked to list three adjectives you would most want others to use when describing you. Do those adjectives highlight your attributes?

Examine your adjectives in terms of you at your best when engaging, inspiring, and motivating others. When you are at your best as a leader or influencer, what strengths are you relying on? What behaviors or actions give you energy? When do people respond to you most positively? Are there attributes not listed you would like to add?

_____

_____

_____

> **Pro Tip:** Your strengths are your superpowers. Embrace them and recognize that what comes naturally to you does not come naturally to everyone.

Value Identification

There are several factors in value alignment. Ask yourself:

- What is valued in the organization?
- What is valued in the role you are in or aspire to?
- What values do you consistently rely on when making ethical choices?

Alignment between the answers to these three questions creates a picture of the values you can embrace and live out day-to-day.

Consistent behaviors concerning those values generate a high level of trust in our authentic leadership. Do you remember 97% of participants who commented on "values in action"? This is how we do it. Exhibiting values in action requires you to:

1 Identify your core values.
2 Model those values.
3 Communicate your values.

Ask yourself:

As a leader, are you explicitly communicating your values with others?
Does your team know what you, as a leader, value in the work?
Do they know what matters to you in terms of relationships, internally and externally?
How do your values align with that of the organization or the work you do?

One question occasionally asked is "What if the values of the department or organization do not align with my personal values anymore?" Incongruence between the organization, its leadership, or a specific task or goal only creates anxiety and stress. When this occurs, leaders must honestly assess whether they can influence positive change within the organization or if maintaining their integrity requires seeking opportunities elsewhere.

Before you can communicate and align, you must become clear about what matters most.

Core Values

We don't often take the time to clarify our core values. The list below provides qualities you may identify as values important to your ability to influence or deliver high-quality outcomes. What do you value? Take a moment to circle the ones that resonate and reflect how you operate.

Acceptance	Diversity	Helping others
Achievement	Economic security	Helping society
Advancement and	Education	Honesty
promotion	Effectiveness	Humor
Adventure	Efficiency	Imagination
Altruism	Elegance	Improvement
Ambition	Entertainment	Independence
Anonymity	Enlightenment	Influencing others
Autonomy	Equality	Innovation
Awareness	Ethics	Inspiration
Balance	Excellence	Integrity
Challenge	Excitement	Intellect
Change	Experiment	Involvement
Community	Expertise	Justice
Competence	Fairness	Knowledge
Competition	Fame	Leadership
Completion	Family	Learning
Connectedness	Happiness	Loyalty
Cooperation	Fast pace	Making a
Collaboration	Freedom	difference
Creativity	Friendship	Mastery
Curiosity	Fun	Meaningful work
Decisiveness	Grace	Money
Design	Growth	Openness
Determination	Harmony	Originality
Discovery	Health	Order

Passion	Relationships	Stability
Peace	Reputation	Status
Personal development	Responsibility and	Success
Personal expression	accountability	Variety
Planning	Respect for others	Warmth
Play	Risk	Wealth
Power	Safety and security	Welcoming
Privacy	Self-respect	environment
Quality	Sensibility	Winning
Questioning	Service	Wisdom
Recognition	Sincerity	

Once you have identified your values, reflect on whether you are currently modeling and communicating those values in an explicit manner. If you see a need to enhance how others perceive your values, think of attitudes, actions, or communication opportunities that would allow you to display and reinforce them.

In Chapter 9, you will learn how to create a leadership advocacy pitch. This is a tool that allows you to create a one-minute pitch highlighting an example of an initiative or project using the STAR (situation, task, action, result) template. Here, you tell a quick story and incorporate language that includes strengths and values where appropriate.

Preparing a leadership advocacy pitch equips you to share, quickly and effectively, a narrative of an accomplishment that can elevate perceptions of executive presence by painting a picture of your abilities and values. An example would be a high-level leader asking you "How are things going in your department?" A small-talk question can turn into an opportunity.

Crafting a Professional Introduction That Resonates

A great everyday opportunity for communicating attributes and values is networking or professional introduction. The standard method of introducing ourselves is to say our name, title, company, and maybe a little about what we do. Your title rarely means anything to the listener. Saying that you are the VP of Procurement does not provide insight into what you do. Rather, find a way to tell a story about who you are, what you do, and why you do it. Create meaning by sharing the results of your work and why you enjoy it or are motivated to do it. This approach allows you to present yourself and your work through the lens of your values and strengths.

Instead, follow this template:

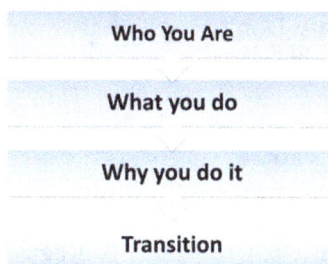

Who You Are

What you do

Why you do it

Transition

Figure 4.1 Introduction framework

Who you are: State your name without your professional title.

What you do: Describe what you do in a way that creates an image of the work and its meaning for the listener. You can state your title as part of the description here or in the next step.

Example: *I work with professionals to empower them to become confident communicators and leaders.*

Why you do it: Tie the purpose of your work to your strengths and values.

Example: *I do this as an executive education faculty member at Johns Hopkins Carey Business School, where my passion for teaching allows me to create high-impact courses for a variety of industry leaders.*

Transition: Shift the conversation back to the other party by asking a relevant question.

Example: *Tell me a little about what you do.*

Talking about yourself and engaging with another, even in short one-on-one interactions, can contribute to perceptions of your executive presence. This type of interaction is a part of not only formulating a strong first impression but also of establishing your personal brand. It involves intentional, strategic practice of defining and expressing your own value proposition.

Pro Tip: A personal introduction is the perfect opportunity to express *what you do and why you do it.* It gives you a way to begin to communicate your strengths, attributes, and values.

Activate—Try It on!

Based on the strengths and values you've identified, complete the following sentences or questions. Don't overthink them, use this as a free writing exercise and see what bubbles up.

1 I am my best, authentic self, when I ...
2 I value other leaders who ...
3 I want to be seen as someone who ...
4 What strengths do I leverage to do my best work?
5 Do I communicate my strengths to my colleagues or team in a way that invites them to bring their strengths to bear on how work gets done?
6 If someone were to ask those who work with me what my strengths are, what might they say?
7 If someone were to ask others what I value most, what might they mention?
8 Am I doing a good job articulating what I value most in work and relationships?
9 What behaviors, attitudes, or actions would demonstrate my values in action?

Notes

1 Gavin R. Dagley and Cadeyrn J. Gaskin, "Understanding Executive Presence: Perspectives of Business Professionals," *Consulting Psychology Journal* 66, no. 3 (2014): 197–211, https://doi.org/10.1037/cpb0000011
2 Gavin R. Dagley and Cadeyrn J. Gaskin, "Understanding Executive Presence: Perspectives of Business Professionals," *Consulting Psychology Journal* 66, no. 3 (2014): 197–211, https://doi.org/10.1037/cpb0000011
3 Sylvia Ann Hewlett, *The New Rules of Executive Presence* (Boston: Harvard Business Review, 2024).
4 Sylvia Ann Hewlett, *The New Rules of Executive Presence* (Boston: Harvard Business Review, 2024).
5 Boas Shamir and Galit Eilam, "What's Your Story? A Life-Stories Approach to Authentic Leadership Development," *Leadership Quarterly* 16 (2005): 395–417.
6 Seyyed Babak Alavi and Carol Gill, "Leading Change Authentically: How Authentic Leaders Influence Follower Responses to Complex Change," *Journal of Leadership & Organizational Studies* 24, no. 2 (2017): 158.

Chapter 5

Emotion Intelligence and Interpersonal Integrity

Inform—Why It Matters

Only 9% of CEOs and 11% of managers consistently demonstrate behaviors associated with moral leadership.[1] This is despite the fact that 95% of employees assess the need for moral leadership as more urgent than ever, according to a 2025 HOW Institute for Society study.[2] Moral leadership is the foundation of interpersonal integrity, and that is at the core of executive presence.

If we assess the need for interpersonal integrity as urgent, why would it seem to be such a difficult thing to come by? We've got two characteristics as humans that can be features or flaws: Emotion and bias. Emotions show us what is important and where to direct our attention. Our cognitive biases help us to efficiently make thousands of decisions that we need to execute on any given day. If let run amok, the combination of the two impairs your thinking, tarnishes your reputation, diminishes your ability to lead effectively. With self-awareness, however, both can be tools that enhance your ability to connect and direct.

> **Pro Tip:** Only a person who is emotionally integrated can lead with integrity.

Step 1: Assess

Emotions

The first step to leveraging your self-awareness is to assess your emotions and determine the status of the needs behind them. Somewhere along the way, we get the message that our emotional world is a risky one and that we can't admit to our needs and still be professional. As a result, we intuit

DOI: 10.4324/9781003624950-7

that acknowledging and dealing with our feelings isn't appropriate at work and may even detract or distract. Yet, as authors Richard Contino and Penelope Holt identify in *Emotional Intelligence at Work:* "Emotional needs, good and bad, are in play across every aspect of the business process."[3] They go on to say that "the party line that emotions have no place in business is self-serving denial."[4] One cannot have interpersonal integrity without grounding it in emotional intelligence.

Our Immense Emotional World

Worse yet, we have trouble assigning the emotions to the needs that gave rise to them in the first place. Our emotions show us what is important, but when, how, and why they show up can be bewildering. What starts as a sensation or an inkling can quickly spiral into a cloud or a funk. Often, we inhabit an emotional state not even knowing what the root is. American psychologist Abraham Maslow developed a theory around our basic needs and their urgency that is often conceptualized as the pyramid seen in Figure 5.1. Table 5.1 is a more recent interpretation by scholars that adds more nuance to the story. These needs motivate the feelings that come up. Aside from our basic needs like clean air, fresh water, healthy food, and stable shelter, we need acceptance, belonging, cooperation, purpose, support, and meaning.

When those needs *are* met, we feel confident, optimistic, proud, energetic, content, and hopeful.

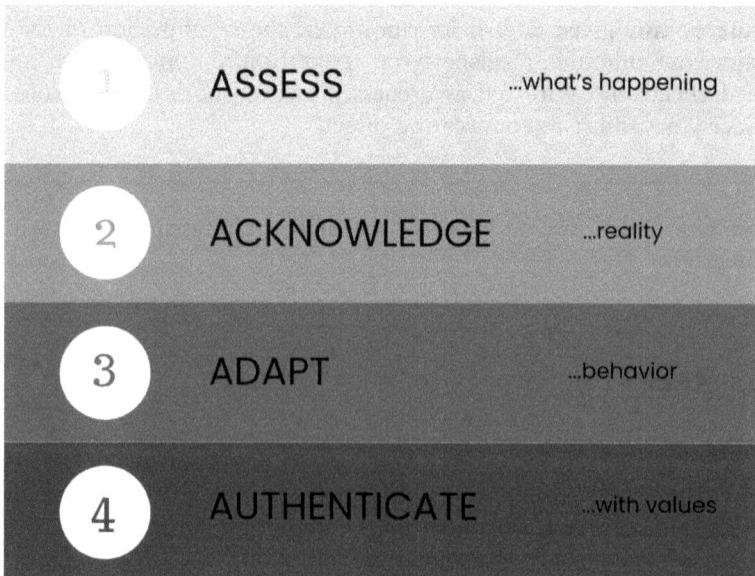

Figure 5.1 Four As framework

Table 5.1 Thirteen fundamental human needs: Concise typology[18]

Need	Facet 1	Facet 2
Autonomy	Volition: Freedom to decide	Individuality: Freedom to express
Beauty	Appeal: Aesthetic pleasure	Harmony: Order and coherence
Comfort	Tranquility: Mental ease	Bodily comfort: Physical ease
Community	Belongingness: Group acceptance	Social harmony: Shared values
Competence	Self-efficacy: Effective functioning	Personal growth: Skill development
Fitness	Mental fitness: Psychological resilience	Physical fitness: Bodily energy
Impact	Influence: Having effect	Contribution: Meaningful input
Morality	Integrity: Living by values	Decency: Experiencing fairness
Purpose	Direction: Clear goals	Spirituality: Deeper meaning
Recognition	Appreciation: Acknowledged value	Respect: Social standing
Relatedness	Closeness: Intimate connection	Care: Trust and support
Security	Safety: Protection from harm	Stability: Predictable conditions
Stimulation	Mental stimulation: Intellectual engagement	Physical stimulation: Sensory engagement

When those needs are *not* met, we may feel angry, resentful, confused, stressed, insecure, exhausted, tired, worried, and annoyed.

Without taking the time to assess the emotion and its likely source, we are prone to reach for the first answer that comes to mind. In an organizational sense, this is easily described in Karl E. Weick and Kathleen Sutcliffe's *Managing the Unexpected: Sustained Performance in a Complex World*, as a "nonobvious breakdown" where we reach for the "first explanation."[5] But this could be a mistake and could indicate proximity rather than accuracy, highlighting a cognitive tendency that we are all prone to. "Identifying and acknowledging hidden emotional motivations or unhelpful tendencies is hard and sometimes painful. In the beginning, it takes a persistent effort,"[6] according to Contino and Holt. In order to make an accurate assessment, it is helpful to acknowledge our biases.

Step 2: Acknowledge

Bias

Bias helps us choose what we want for dinner and what is the best way to get it. Relying on our experience or perception, it is an efficient way to make thinking shortcuts that prevent cognitive overload from thousands of decisions we must make during any given day. Bias allows us to go with what we know (experience bias); it prompts us to go with the flow (convenience bias); or sometimes it inspires us to just say "no" (negative bias). The risk with bias is that it helps us to bridge over any gap in our knowledge with confidence (confidence bias) and that can undermine our integrity. If favoritism is suspected in your leadership, that can really disenchant those we are tasked to lead. Similarly, if you reach for the solution that worked before, only because it is familiar, without considering other perspectives that might have an innovative insight to offer, you could discourage teammates and employees who would otherwise have a lot to offer.

Step 3: Adapt

Once you have assessed your emotions and acknowledged any biases, you have an opportunity to adapt your thinking or actions with what you discovered. Challenging your own assumptions in this way and making space to deeply listen to other points of view can be a powerful tool.

Build Trust through Supportive Engagement

According to organizational anthropologist Judith Glaser, "we trust those who care about us and are fair, are clear on ownership of tasks and responsibilities, reciprocate, cooperate, give us space and time to express what's on our mind, and value our contributions."[7] These kind of interactions can be described as supportive engagement. Even in conversation, our neurochemistry supports these moments. When participating in supportive engagement we release oxytocin, the chemical for social bonding, as well as dopamine and serotonin, which add to our feeling of well-being.[8] Most likely, this aligns with your values, how you want to treat others, and how you want to be treated.

> **Pro Tip:** One cannot *not* communicate.

Our habitual responses, however, can get in the way. Your brain assesses the threat or safety of a situation with .07 seconds.[9] In just that short period, our cortisol levels will go up, causing the heart to beat faster if our "protect/fear network" is activated or, alternatively, our "trust network" can release those feel-good chemicals. If you are pulled into a protect/fear response, you are also less likely to act from your core values. Worse yet, once triggered, cortisol remains in the blood stream. Normally, it has a 26-hour time span, but continuing to dwell on the interaction, or ruminate, can trigger more cortisol, effectively keeping you in a doom loop.[10]

To avoid that response, we can follow the model that is already inherent within us: Being open to adaptation. Our vestibular system is the one that keeps us balanced and upright. That internal compass is always processing new information in real time and recalibrating in response. What if our body's automatic response to gravity could inspire our own gravitas? Physical balance requires all of our systems working together; interpersonal integrity requires calibrating self-awareness, authenticity, empathy, and context at the same time. For professionals that means being aware of our emotions, speaking honestly about them. With that sense of self-assurance, we are able to inspire others to engage similarly.

Step 4: Authenticate

The final step in the process is grounding any action you take or words you say in your core values. This is how you ensure that your actions align with the impact you want to make, and do so over a long period of time. But sometimes this is easier said than done. Authenticity is not a zero-sum game, especially when it comes to executive presence. Although we all subtly adjust our communication strategies depending on the situation and the audience, some changes can feel more drastic than others.

Code Switching

Code switching is assessing the landscape and calculating which set of behaviors you'll use strategically. It is an opportunity to ensure that you are moving in alignment with your aspirations.[11] In a sense, it is about orientation, not location. What matters is where you want to go with your career and the cultural norms of that place. If those norms differ from your home environment, you have the ability to translate yourself and your thoughts into the language that would be most readily understood to achieve your goal. This demonstrates cognitive flexibility and self-efficacy. Oftentimes, it's unconscious, but it is also a skill that can be developed. This agility comes not from a lack of authenticity, but perhaps knowing yourself so well that you understand the many different parts of you and can translate them into action. It can be an essential part of a boundaryless career that displays comfort and mobility across physical and psychological barriers.[12]

International management expert Andy Molinsky recommends using six dimensions to determine how best to align yourself into the culture of your target. These are directness, enthusiasm, formality, assertiveness, self-promotion, and self-disclosure.[13] He also says that one of the biggest sticking points is that we often imagine someone from back home judging us as we assimilate to get ahead. But intersectionality theory celebrates how we are able to inhabit multiple identities at once, and postmodern identity theory shows us how our identities are fluid, multifaceted, and context-dependent. Think of one of the many cities in the world with multicultural workforces, and many different languages spoken at home. In such a place, adapting and adopting are the keys to interpersonal communication.

Pro Tip: Say what you mean, and mean what you say.

Putting It All Together

When tapping into your emotional intelligence to demonstrate interpersonal integrity using the 4As framework, you are directing your movements from your core values. Not only are you articulating them, you are also clearly embodying them. Remember, communication is not just what you say, it is how you act and move as well, as discussed in Chapters 3 and 4. This points to Chapters 7 and 8. Steadily balancing toward a style that communicates your values, and away from those that don't, signals a powerful form of integrity. Now, from this grounded place of emotional integration, you enter interactions from a more self-regulated and less reactive state. Your direction is intentional and the impression you leave is more reliable. This is integrity in action.

Equip—Skills or Behaviors That Enhance the Area in Focus

Listening

Deep Listening

The most fundamental skill to refining your emotional intelligence and by extension, your interpersonal integrity, is listening. We hear lots of information, and tune most of it out as a natural consequence, but that is the opposite of being present. To listen deeply, even to yourself, requires an intentionality around the process. This practice, which has ancient roots in many cultures, is the perfect method to enhance well-being and coherence. It turns out that deep listening and being open to the ideas that spark around us is at the essence of executive presence as well. It instills trust in our leadership. The research on deep listening shows that it improves cognitive function and allows us access to our prefrontal cortex, rather than keeping us trapped in the amygdala area of our brain, prone to reactivity.[14] Listening to yourself requires just as much focus as listening to others. Indeed, the two are intimately connected, as mentioned earlier. Human attention is a powerful resource and the currency of trust. Build trust by identifying obstacles that can get in the way of listening and resolving them before engaging in listening.

Some of the obstacles that impede our listening include:

- We have too much to do.
- We have too much to say.
- We have too little interest.
- We have too much distraction or apathy.
- We have too much technology in the way.[15]

Listening presence

- Identify any obstacle that could keep you from fully listening.
- Identify the reason you are listening.[16]
- Suspend judgment.[17]
- Get curious: Cultivate an attitude of discovery.
- Paraphrase.
- Pretend you don't know anything.

Emotions

Naming

To access your full emotional intelligence, it is helpful to:

- Name the sensation that surfaces.
- Assign a feeling.
- Recognize the need that it connects to.
- Create an action plan to address it.

List of Human Needs

Recognizing your needs, when they are met, and when they are unmet, are the first steps to embracing emotion and incorporating them into your integrity. Maslow's Hierarchy of Needs, as seen in Figure 5.2, is an excellent starting point for recognizing our requirements for well-being.

However, researchers have further developed those theories and added more nuance to what it takes to thrive. Researchers Pieter Desmet and Steven Fokkinga identified a wider range of fundamental needs that can influence our emotions in Table 5.1.

Label Your Emotions

Just by assigning names to them you can increase the intensity of positive emotions and help regulate the intensity of negative emotions.[19] This is a powerful processing tool that empowers you with the agency to improve your emotional intelligence by knowing what is going on within you. It allows you to audit your motivations before entering a conversation or negotiation, so you can prioritize the desired outcome.

Code Switching

The necessity to code switch can be fraught with self-doubt and can challenge your own sense of authenticity. While it can present a psychological cost when unacknowledged, targeted use can be beneficial,

Maslow's Hierarchy of Needs

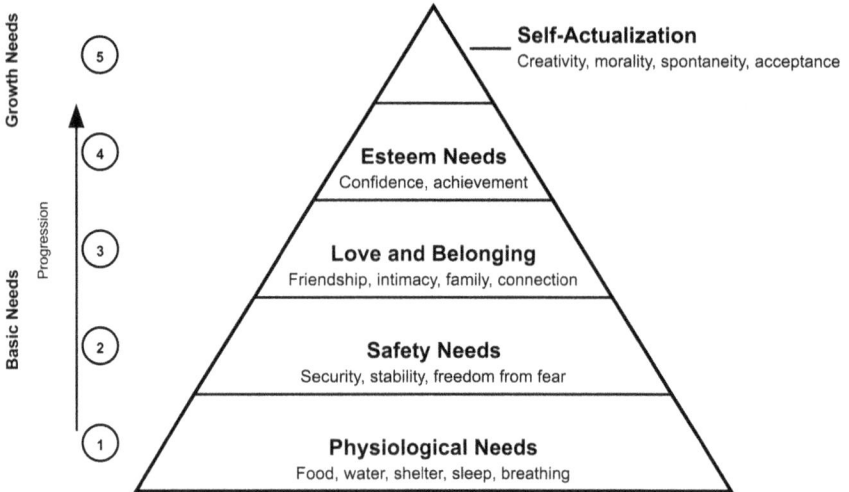

Figure 5.2 Maslow's hierarchy of needs

setting up healthy boundaries. You can also gain new clarity, insights, and perspectives by activating your ability to code switch in these different ways. Exercise your agency by translating your communication for different audiences in your life and professional sphere. Try on the following mindsets and determine which one fits best to your goals when code switching.

Table 5.2 Labeling your emotions when needs are met

Category	Representative feelings
Affectionate	Compassionate, loving, tender, warm
Confident	Empowered, proud, safe, secure
Engaged	Curious, fascinated, involved, stimulated
Excited	Animated, giddy, passionate, vibrant
Exhilarated	Blissful, ecstatic, radiant, thrilled
Grateful	Appreciative, moved, thankful, touched
Hopeful	Encouraged, expectant, optimistic, inspired
Joyful	Amused, glad, happy, tickled
Peaceful	Calm, centered, relaxed, serene
Refreshed	Rejuvenated, renewed, rested, revived

Table 5.3 Labeling your emotions when needs are not met[20]

Category	Representative feelings
Afraid	Apprehensive, frightened, scared, worried
Annoyed	Aggravated, frustrated, impatient, irked
Angry	Enraged, furious, outraged, resentful
Aversion	Disgusted, hostile, repulsed, horrified
Confused	Baffled, bewildered, hesitant, puzzled
Disconnected	Alienated, apathetic, distant, withdrawn
Disquiet	Agitated, alarmed, perturbed, uneasy
Embarrassed	Ashamed, chagrined, flustered, mortified
Fatigue	Exhausted, lethargic, tired, worn out
Pain	Hurt, lonely, miserable, heartbroken
Sad	Depressed, discouraged, hopeless, gloomy
Tense	Anxious, nervous, overwhelmed, stressed
Vulnerable	Fragile, insecure, sensitive, helpless
Yearning	Longing, nostalgic, envious, wistful

Table 5.4 Code switch reframe

Rename	Rewrite	Redirect	Reposition
Refrain	Repurpose	Respond	Relate
Regain	Relocate	Release	Renew

Activate

Try This

Flex Your Listening Muscle

1 Take a walk at night in a quiet place where you feel safe and comfortable.
2 Walk so silently that your feet become ears.[21]
3 What do you notice about the act of listening?

Follow the Leader

• Who comes to mind when you think of a leader who simultaneously embodies emotional intelligence and interpersonal integrity?
• How do they make these qualities legible? Be specific.

Emotional Audit

• Review: How did emotions drive your decision-making this week?
• Investigate: What are some reset mechanisms, or activities that clear your mind, that work particularly well for you?

- Create: Draw a map, calendar, or schedule of your emotions. When and where do certain feelings crop up?
- Implement: Craft an executive message that embraces emotion.

Spaces, Places, Faces Audit

- Who is influencing my emotions?
- Who am I around most of the day?
- Which environments or people have the most influence on how I feel?

Narrative Processing

1 Set a timer for five minutes.
2 Start your recording device.
3 Talk through a time in your life when you have gone through adversity.
4 Listen to the recording.
5 Name the sensations that are evoked when listening to your story (e.g., heaviness, buzzing, warmth, tightness).
6 Locate where those sensations are the strongest (chest, shoulders, head, throat, etc.).
7 Assign emotions to each of those sensations.

Biofeedback Hack

1 Place one hand on your heart to feel your heart beat.
2 Place the other hand on your belly to feel the movement of the torso with the breath.
3 Release your hands while maintaining awareness of those two rhythms within the body.
4 Walk around your favorite place to get fresh air.
5 Narrate each step.
6 Keep adding more minute detail about what you are doing (e.g., my right foot is landing, my left arm is swinging).
7 Narrate the information being taken in through your senses:

   a Name everything that you can see.
   b Name everything you can smell.
   c List the sounds that you hear.
   d Categorize sensations of touch:

      i What do your clothes feel like on your skin?
      ii Notice the pressure of each part of the foot as you move.

   e What can you taste?

8 If you find your mind wandering to your to-do list, acknowledge this and redirect the focus back to the present moment.
9 Reflect: What did this activity bring into your awareness?

Code Switch Sitch

Use a mirror or find a friend.

1 Think of an important and possibly difficult conversation you have coming up.
2 Practice delivering the information in drastically different ways:

a Informally, as if you are hanging out with close friends.
b Formally in front of leadership.

3 Notice how your body changes with the different styles of communication.
4 Record yourself doing this.
5 Gain dexterity with switching between both styles of communicating.
6 Assess your bio feedback.
7 Reflect: Which communication style makes you feel more activated?

Notes

1 Dov Seidman, *The State of Moral Leadership in Business*, 2025. https://the-howinstitute.org/state-of-moral-leadership-in-business-2025/
2 Dov Seidman, *The State of Moral Leadership in Business*, 2025. https://the-howinstitute.org/state-of-moral-leadership-in-business-2025/
3 Richard M. Contino and Penelope J. Holt, *Emotional Intelligence at Work : A Personal Operating System for Career Success*, 1st ed. (New York: Business Expert Press, 2021).
4 Richard M. Contino and Penelope J. Holt, *Emotional Intelligence at Work : A Personal Operating System for Career Success*, 1st ed. (New York: Business Expert Press, 2021).
5 Karl E. Weick and Kathleen M. Sutcliffe, *Managing the Unexpected : Resilient Performance in an Age of Uncertainty,*2nd ed. (San Francisco: Jossey-Bass, 2007).
6 Richard M. Contino and Penelope J. Holt, *Emotional Intelligence at Work : A Personal Operating System for Career Success*, 1st ed. (New York: Business Expert Press, 2021).
7 Judith E. Glaser, *Conversational Intelligence: How Great Leaders Build Trust and Get Extraordinary Results*, 1st ed. (New York: Routledge, 2016), chap. 8. https://doi.org/10.4324/9781315230443
8 Judith E. Glaser, *Conversational Intelligence: How Great Leaders Build Trust and Get Extraordinary Results*, 1st ed. (New York: Routledge, 2016), chap. 8. https://doi.org/10.4324/9781315230443
9 Judith E. Glaser, *Conversational Intelligence: How Great Leaders Build Trust and Get Extraordinary Results*, 1st ed. (New York: Routledge, 2016), chap. 3. https://doi.org/10.4324/9781315230443

10 Judith E. Glaser, *Conversational Intelligence: How Great Leaders Build Trust and Get Extraordinary Results*, 1st ed. (New York: Routledge, 2016), chap. 7. https://doi.org/10.4324/9781315230443

11 Angela Danielle Carter and Stephanie Sisco, "Leadership Coaching Strategies for Black Women Leaders Who Code Switch: Avoiding Linguistic Profiling Career Boundaries," *Career Development International* 29, no. 3 (2024), 323–338. https://doi.org/10.1108/CDI-07-2023-0211

12 Sherry E. Sullivan and Michael B. Arthur, "The Evolution of the Boundaryless Career Concept: Examining Physical and Psychological Mobility," *Journal of Vocational Behavior* 69, no. 1 (2006), 19–29. https://doi.org/10.1016/j.jvb.2005.09.001

13 Andy Molinsky and Sarah Cliffe, "'Companies Don't Go Global, People do': An Interview with Andy Molinsky," *Harvard Business Review* 93, no. 10 (2015), 82–85.

14 Judith E. Glaser, *Conversational Intelligence: How Great Leaders Build Trust and Get Extraordinary Results*, 1st ed. (New York: Routledge, 2016), sec. Introduction. https://doi.org/10.4324/9781315230443

15 Marcel Robles, *The Importance of Listening in Strategic Communication/ Marcel Robles* (Los Angeles, CA: SAGE Publications, Inc., 2023).

16 Judith E. Glaser, *Conversational Intelligence: How Great Leaders Build Trust and Get Extraordinary Results*, 1st ed. (New York: Routledge, 2016), chap. 8. https://doi.org/10.4324/9781315230443.

17 Judith E. Glaser, *Conversational Intelligence: How Great Leaders Build Trust and Get Extraordinary Results*, 1st ed. (New York: Routledge, 2016), sec. Introduction. https://doi.org/10.4324/9781315230443.

18 Pieter Desmet and Steven Fokkinga, "Beyond Maslow's Pyramid: Introducing a Typology of Thirteen Fundamental Needs for Human-Centered Design," *Multimodal Technologies and Interaction* 4, no. 3 (2020), 38–22. https://doi.org/10.3390/mti4030038

19 Valeriia V. Vlasenko, Emma G. Rogers and Christian E. Waugh, "Affect Labelling Increases the Intensity of Positive Emotions," *Cognition and Emotion* 35, no. 7 (2021), 1350–1364. https://doi.org/10.1080/02699931.2021.1959302

20 "Feelings/Emotions Partial List,", accessed May 22, 2025, https://thefearless-heart.org/nvc-reference-materials/list-of-feelings/

21 Pauline Oliveros, "Meditation V," in *Sonic Meditations* (Kingston, NY: PoPand MoM Publications, 2022).

Chapter 6

Overcoming Limiting Beliefs

Inform—Why It Matters

According to a 2024 Korn Ferry Workforce Survey, 71% of CEOs interviewed identified feelings of impostor syndrome in their roles.[1] However, CEOs are not the only ones affected; high-achieving professionals commonly experience feelings of fraudulence or inadequacy at every level. Somehow, despite the objective evidence to the contrary, there are times when it is hard to believe they've earned their success legitimately.[2] This is a limiting belief.

The Inner Critic

The term impostor phenomenon (IP), alternatively called impostor syndrome, was first coined by researchers Pauline Rose Clance and Suzanne Ament Imes in their 1978 research. They were surprised at the prevalence of successful women expressing feelings of self-doubt. Since then, research has revealed gender and race, as well as socioeconomic and parenting status can influence IP.[3] However, as the tools to measure and treat IP have developed more sophistication, a trend is emerging that shows increasing frequency in rates of occurrence across multiple demographics. In fact, according to Korn Ferry's study, the sentiments of self-questioning affect both male and female professionals at similar rates.[4]

First, let's recognize some of the common signs of the impostor phenomenon:

- Rejection sensitivity
- Depressed entitlement
- Perfectionism
- Intellectual self-doubt
- Low self-esteem
- Feeling of fraudulence

DOI: 10.4324/9781003624950-8

- Feelings of inadequacy
- Denial or failure to internalize competencies, accolades, achievements, or successes
- Depression
- Burnout
- Excessive comparison to peers

Considering that the National Science Foundation found that the human brain generates as many as 50,000 thoughts a day, and 95% of those are repeated, it is easy to see how limiting beliefs, such as impostor syndrome, could affect one's performance, interactions, and quality of life.[5] The truth is, "everyone is susceptible to negative self-talk and self-doubt, particularly when we allow ourselves to suffer in isolation."[6] The expertise needed to fulfill the many tasks required of us in a single day can make anyone, especially the most senior leaders, feel overwhelmed and underprepared. Similarly, the higher up the professional ladder they climb, the harder it is to believe that such a steep ascent can be attributed to their ability alone.

Trait vs. State

Current research around IP recognizes that it can surface unexpectedly after lying dormant or it can accompany professionals as a consistent trait.[7] Some might feel its impact more acutely when triggered by an event; others experience IP in every professional interaction. To begin dissecting this a bit further, it is helpful to categorize where the ideas that foster imposter syndrome emanate from. There can be a lot of complexity with detecting the origin of a thought. For our purposes, we will simplify this into two categories: those that stem from an *internal* thought or feeling, and those that stem from some sort of *external* message that we interpret and internalize.

With these two categories in mind, some situations that trigger the feeling of imposter syndrome are displayed in Table 6.1[8,9]

Table 6.1 Sources of imposter phenomenon

Internal	External
Having a fixed mindset	New environment
Needing help	Discrimination
Applied learning	Evaluations
Challenging new role	Peer comparisons
Lack of belonging	The status of the perceiver

Beliefs

Wherever the ideas originate from, once we adopt them, they become beliefs and this matters whether it is temporary as a state or something that becomes a more stable belief, which acts like a trait. The beliefs become the origins of impostor syndrome. Think about the first day at a new job, the belief "I don't fit in here" can start as a temporary internal belief that is quickly dispelled by the culture and community in the office of warmth and welcome. In that case, you can adapt a new belief in response to this new information. But imagine coming in with that same belief "I don't fit in here," and being subject to the cold shoulder from most of the people in the office, or worse yet, a lack of cooperation, discrimination, and a resulting poor performance evaluation. In this case, once that belief is confirmed, it could reinforce other doubts and lead to a crippling result.

Beliefs are developed in response to early experiences, culture, and society, but can be strengthened or weakened over time. The brain adopts and adapts core beliefs as survival responses to keep us safe. By limiting us, the brain is working to keep us safe from the threat any risk could bring. We recognize that each new opportunity comes with new vulnerabilities. Since the brain acts as a predictor, it is constantly scanning the environment for confirming evidence and rewarding the nervous system with dopamine when it's found. As crazy as it might sound, impostor syndrome is rewarding the body through a chemical high by protecting you from any discomfort that could accompany the chance you might fail. As psychologist Brian Little explains in *Me, Myself, and Us,* our beliefs can serve as both "frames and cages."[10]

Such a well-worn path is not easy to shift. Any change to a well-established belief framework requires the brain to do much more work than it wants to, so it resists, and protects itself through outputs like distraction, exhaustion, and depression. It is important to note that creating lasting change requires a comprehensive strategy employing both physical pathways and cognitive reinforcements.[11]

Transform

The "frequency, intensity, and disruptive impact" of IP can vary across populations and people.[12] Detecting where it shows its impact can help you create and sustain the best intervention for yourself. You can start that investigation with the limiting belief audit in the Activate section of this chapter. Once you have identified some of those beliefs, it is time to consider how you can transform them.

Mindfulness behavior interventions have been developed in the field of clinical psychology over the past 40 years and have proven their effectiveness through the scientific method. Skills that help include present-moment awareness, decentering, and acceptance.[13] Neuroimaging studies have shown that contemplative practices, such as meditation, are capable of changing the connectivity patterns in the brain. This allows for improvements around attention, self-processing, rumination, and interoception (sensing what you are feeling) by having an impact on positive mental well-being.[14] Simply recognizing, naming, discussing, and seeking to understand this phenomenon can make a big difference. The strategies below help to lay new pathways of thinking and being while allowing non-desired ones to weaken.

Psychological Skills of Executive Presence

When limiting beliefs overcome us, we don't think we are capable of dealing with the task at hand. We focus on the reasons that emphasize we are *not* capable and ignore all the objective reasons that we are. This distracted state can be deflating and debilitating. It can cause procrastination and avoidance. Instead of being present we are pushed toward absence. But, there have been moments when everything clicked, where you said the right words, finished the task on time, made the right joke, and made a good impression. Not only were you embodying executive presence in those moments, you were also likely in a state of *flow*.

In *Flow 2.0: Optimal Experience in a Complex World, Honoring Mihaly Csikszentmihalyi's Legacy*, Steward Donaldson and Matthew Dubin build on the Csikszentmihalyi work to define *flow* as a "complete immersion and energized focus on a singular endeavor."[15] Being in flow is a kind of superhuman state where you are in the zone, or in the groove, and nothing else matters or distracts you from the task at hand.

While watching the Olympics, it is amazing to see how similar the interviews with the winning athletes are. Inevitably, the interviewer explains the significance of the achievement and then question the athlete with a probing "How did that feel?" or "What was going on in your mind when …?" Time after time, the newly crowned winner offers a version of "I don't know," "I'm still processing," or "I just stuck to the plan." Were these athletes not thinking? They just demonstrated lightning-fast reactions and precise maneuvering around obstacles and opponents, some predictable, but others unforeseeable. How can they not expect these questions and be ready to boast about what they'd just done in detail?

It seems that the intense state of *flow* that they access to win is not so easily shaken off, and it takes much longer before they can return to an analytical style of thinking and being. They are embodying peak performance. Luckily this sense of flow is a capacity that resides in all of us even without extensive physical training. Think about the last time you talked for an hour with a friend, not realizing how much time had passed, or lost track of time while experiencing a sublime form of art. Consistently accessing this state during stressful situations, however, takes skill and planning.

Sports psychology has discovered how important it is to coordinate psychological skills while training athletes, so that they can get out of their own way and do their best work. Utilizing these techniques can improve your ability to act in high-pressure situations as well. Author Matt Abrahams advocates for everyone to have what he calls an "anxiety management plan" or AMP.[16] Because anxiety is a natural response to high-pressure situations, it can be expected and planned for. In fact, the hormone release that is often characterized as nervousness is similar to the one we feel when describing the feelings of excitement.[17] Alison Wood Brooks designed an innovative study that directed participants to say "I am excited" out loud, before completing anxiety-producing tasks: Singing, speaking, and doing math in public. Her experiment, with over 300 participants, found that although heart rate remained high throughout the task, reappraising pre-performance anxiety as excitement, as compared to anxiety or calmness, improved the subsequent performance by priming an *opportunity* mindset.[18]

Habit, best described as the input of automated learning and output of automated recall, works well in laboratory settings, but under stress this coordination can quickly fall apart. The following skills provide beacons where professionals can guide themselves with tactical precision when dealing with stress that could otherwise undermine them.

Equip—Skills or Behaviors That Enhance the Area in Focus

Let's talk through each of these psychological skills that can help overcome limiting beliefs and enhance access to peak performance:

- Relaxation/Regulation
- Self-talk
- Imagery
- Goal setting
- Concentration

Relaxation/Regulation

Cognitive affective stress management training applies empirically supported methods of cognitive and somatic coping skills. These types of interventions have proved effective in clinical and nonclinical populations, including stressed-out medical students, military officers in demanding training programs, and athletes who identified stress as a negative predictor of performance.[19] The goal is to empower you with the ability to learn how to self-regulate emotions during stressful situations.[20]

If you are thinking you can skip this section because you don't experience stress, you are not alone. Researchers Ronald Smith and James Ascough found that some of their clients did not comply with their relaxation training because they believed they didn't experience high forms of physiological arousal.[21] Their high level of baseline tension had become so normalized to them that it didn't stick out; it barely seemed worth addressing. However, this same population later reported that cognitive affective stress management training had positive effects for them. Mindfulness interventions have been found to make a measurable positive difference on the physiological markers such as resting heart rate and cortisol levels, as well as psychological factors, like anxiety, that directly influence performance.[22] The goal of relaxation techniques is to help you turn muscles on and off as needed, recognize unnecessary tensions, and prevent the distraction of anxiety welling up in the body.[23]

Regulation techniques offer another way to think about maintaining your calm in stressful situations. This puts you in a place where you can respond to the situation at hand—and only the situation at hand. Melissa Romano, in the Vagus Nerve Deck of exercise cards, says that with regulation, "a more comprehensive definition is to be in connection with yourself—to feel aligned in your mind and body, safe in your surroundings, and connected to others."[24]

Self-Talk

Self-talk is the skill of improving how you talk to yourself. We'll discuss the nature of the inner voice more in Chapter 8, but for now just think of anything that might go through your head before, during, and after a demanding situation. When strategically employed to deliberately achieve an outcome, self-talk can "enhance individual performance," and boost "skill execution, self-efficacy, and focus of attention while reducing performance anxiety."[25]

In order to hone this skill, Richard Gerson, in *The Executive Athlete*, advises professionals to "look for a trigger word that will ignite the resource-full self in you whenever you need it (e.g., power, pump, the best, get busy, bam, yes!, strong, now!).[26] The benefit of motivating and cueing your own self-talk when seeking peak performance is that it allows you to write your own script. You are putting your conscious mind in a powerful position and into the director's chair. You can choose the words that go through your mind.

To get started, consider how you want to feel when you are in peak performance mode and experiencing success in your domain. Get very specific and explicit about that, perhaps drawing on successful moments in recent history. Take some time to jot down the adjectives that best describe you while you are in that mode and some verbs that closely relate to getting you into that zone. Once you are clear on these adjectives, you can remind yourself of these words and plan how to feel to cue your goal-directed self-talk.

> **Pro Tip:** We can tell an alternative story.

Imagery

Now, for the fun part: In addition to talking yourself through what success feels like through self-talk, you can utilize imagery to mentally experience your success through visualization. Your mind has a powerful ability to control action. According to sports psychologist Kate F. Hays, "many top professional athletes have learned to hone this affirmative competence, projecting detailed positive guiding images as if they were already true."[27]

This effect has been seen in other areas also. A study published in 2022 found that training would-be entrepreneurs with imagery as well as business training led to stronger and more sustained economic outcomes.[28] This effect was even stronger among those with high levels of baseline trauma as the researchers hypothesized that the training in positive imagery was able to address a deficit that existed within that sub-group unbeknownst to them.

When accessing this skill, there are some guidelines that have been found to improve efficacy. Make sure that your visualization is:

Multisensory: Use your senses of sight, smell, hearing, taste, and touch to put yourself to get as close to reality as possible in the situation you'd like to thrive in.

Vivid: Perceive the situation with as much detail as possible. Even silly things that you can imagine like the exact time on the clock can help make a vivid picture in your mind's eye. Think about the time of day and the faces that might be in the room with you.

Sequential: Proceed in the order things will likely take place. This allows you to establish and integrate flow.

Complete: Go from beginning to end and avoid interruptions to your imagery. The temptation to fragment and get distracted is a big one, but that would be rehearsing getting interrupted rather than rehearsing successful completion of the targeted task.

Informed: Utilize the information available to you to create the most detailed picture possible. Think about all of the details that will go into the targeted task. If the space is unknown to you, find a picture online. If there is none available, use your imagination. Surely you will be able to imagine many of the important aspects that will make your mental rehearsal more thorough.

Emotive: As demonstrated in Chapter 5 and by the 2022 study with entrepreneurs cited earlier, emotions matter. They are an important part of the human experience. Practice imagining what emotional success on this very important topic will be. Refer back to Table 5.2 to get an idea of which emotions you would like to choose.

Goal Setting

Goal setting is a tool to help you stay moving toward your target, but not just any goals will do.[29] SMART goals were described earlier in the book. The acronym stands for Specific, Measurable, Assignable, Realistic, and Time-related, and has been a helpful guidepost even as the meanings of some letters have shifted over the years.

- Specific
- Measurable
- Achievable (but challenging)
- Relevant
- Time-based (limited)

A helpful addition to that list is:

- Adjustable
- Fulfilling

While the first five are self-explanatory to anyone reading this book and intent on improving their executive presence, the last two could use an explanation as they tap into some of the latest developments in psychology. Our goals benefit from being *adjustable* as a way to engage cognitive flexibility. When our goals are adjustable, we give ourselves permission to realize their essence in multiple ways. Think of knowing multiple routes to get home depending on the time of day. Goal setting with the capacity to recognize alternatives as equally fulfilling or rewarding opens up a range of options to satisfy the achievement, some of which might only reveal themselves as the situation unfolds. Imagine setting a goal of being promoted in your current organization when a conversation with a colleague leads to a better offer at a different organization. Adjusting expectations can lead to an improved quality of life.

When done well, goals hold some sort of intrinsic meaning that makes them worth pursuing.[30] That means when we accomplish them, or in our adjusted frame, something similar, it is worth recognizing and celebrating. Finding reward in the goal can be a helpful motivating factor, and planning to celebrate the accomplishment even more so. Too often, we diminish the value of our achievements by not being present with their magnitude, and instead focusing on the next mountain to climb. This sets up a negative feedback loop. We are training our brain that the reward for hard work is just more hard work. Scaffolding a sense of fulfillment from the outset and prioritizing time to celebrate sets a positive example and retrains your brain to utilize positive psychology to achieve results.

Concentration

The last skill of the canon of psychological skill training ties relaxation/regulation, self-talk, imagery, and goal setting together. We live in a distracted world—but our ability to concentrate still has incredible value. Our awareness of the clock, the calendar, the phone, and the watch snips away at our concentration. In her bestselling 2020 book, *Overwhelmed: Work, Love and Play When No One Has the Time*, Brigid Schulte coined the term *time confetti* for this phenomenon of split attention that leads to a feeling a depletion.[31] It turns out, concentration, like all of these mental skills, is also a muscle that can be trained through repetition. Here are some activities to try it on.

Activate—Activities That Allow You to Try It on

Limiting Belief Audit

Impostor syndrome often shows up through specific patterns of thinking and behavior that undermine confidence. This activity helps you identify those patterns and examine how they limit your effectiveness and sense of self.

1 List the three limiting beliefs from or impostor behaviors listed in the Inform section that most affect you.
2 For each behavior, list examples of when they commonly arise, adding history and context.
3 List their impact on your work and life.
4 Put objective parameters around the situation by looking at it from a different point of view.

  a What might an outsider notice when looking at the same situation?

Real Strengths Audit

Purpose: Identify and intentionally use your core character strengths to boost confidence and positive emotions before high-pressure situations. Research shows that using signature strengths in new ways increases happiness and performance.

Part 1: Identify Your Signature Strengths

- Take the VIA Character Strengths Survey at www.viasurvey.org (free). This assessment identifies your top five character strengths from 24 universal traits.
- Alternative: If you can't access the survey, reflect on these questions:
  - What do people consistently compliment you on?
  - When do you feel most authentically yourself?
  - What activities energize rather than drain you?
  - What strengths do you use when you're at your best?

Part 2: Make a Plan

Imagine how you could use your top three signature strengths, each one in new ways, this week.

Professional applications

- Notice how this strength looks when you are:
  - Leading meetings
  - Presenting
  - Holding difficult conversations
  - Collaborating
- What is better when leading with this strength?

Pre-performance applications

- How could you activate this strength:
  - Before a big presentation?
  - During networking?
  - Handling workplace stress?

Part 3: The One-Week Challenge

Each day for one week:

1 Choose one signature strength to focus on.
2 Use it in a new way you haven't tried before.
3 Apply it to a work situation (meeting, email, conversation, problem-solving).
4 Notice the impact on your mood, confidence, and performance.

Daily tracking:

- Strength used: _____
- New application: _____
- Situation: _____
- How it felt: _____
- Impact on performance: _____

Part 4: Executive Presence Integration

After your week of practice, identify:

1 Which strength most boosted your confidence?
2 Which applications felt most natural in professional settings?
3 How can you build these into your regular routine?
4 What's your "go-to" strength for high-stakes situations?

Bonus Application: Before your next important presentation or meeting, spend two to three minutes intentionally activating your strongest signature strength. Notice how this affects your presence and performance.

Failure Resume

Recognizing failures can provide a more complete account of the time, effort, and energy you've put into achieving your goals. This acknowledgment helps address imposter syndrome through objective evidence of a gradual journey to your current level of success.

1 Create a detailed CV with all of the times you've failed. You can list:

    a Colleges you didn't into (or were too scared to apply to)
    b Interviews you didn't get
    c Jobs you didn't get hired for
    d Projects that collapsed
    e Promotions you got passed over for

2 Quantify the time you put into each one of those projects.
3 Qualify the effort and aspirations involved with each one.
4 Compare your *Failure Resume* and your *Success Resume*.
5 Notice the connections and the causality between the two.
6 Identify moments of:

    a Resilience
    b Learning
    c Growth

7 Think about how you can metabolize that story through reframing.

 a What unexpected benefits came?
 b What other pathways did you discover?
 c What did you learn about yourself? These are the most compelling stories.

8 Think about an upcoming situation that might result in success or failure.

 a First, evaluate the likelihood of both with as much objective evidence as available.

  i What is the actual likelihood of those worse case scenarios?

 b Do a five-minute free-write on what could go right.
 c Think of both practical positive impacts, but also let your imagination run wild with the possibility.
 d How does it feel when you meditate on these thoughts?
 e If it feels good that can be an important feeling to harness when you step into that room.

Deep Flow Audit

Sometimes finding deep flow can feel illusive. Paradoxically, the professional environment can be a great place to find flow because of the structure, clear goals, feedback, and dedicated time allotted to certain engaging tasks.[32] As you begin the process of cultivating flow as a pathway to peak performance, tap into your personal experience with the phenomenon to show the way.

1 Think about a time you were engaged in an activity that brought about deep flow.

 a Absorbed
 b Energized
 c Lost track of time

2 Describe the conditions that contributed to finding that state. Some helpful things to consider are:

 a Structure/Boundaries
 b Time of day
 c Location
 d Routine
 e People/Colleagues

3 Notice which patterns emerge from this list.

4 Create rituals that create the conditions that can lead to flow.
5 Connect those discoveries to demanding situations you will encounter that could benefit from flow.

Pro Tip: Practice in safe settings and in low-stakes situations until new patterns feel authentic.[33]

Sharpen Psychological Skills

The psychological skills we discussed earlier can continue to be sharpened over your professional career to account for new situations and challenges. Use these suggestions to adapt the skills to your values, vision, and voice.

- Relaxation/Regulation
  - Purposefully design spaces, activities into the work flow that allow you to balance stressors with soothers.
- Self-talk
  - Reframe situations that trigger anxiety by contemplating best-case scenarios and what could go right.
    - "The most empirically supported individual-focused interventions rely on cognitive reframing and retraining strategies to address maladaptive, self-critical cognitive distortions."[34]
  - Listen for negative voices or doom loops in your head, then interrupt those cycles.
    - Interrogate those voices.
    - Add objective information to quiet them.
- Imagery
  - Visualize success. See what you will look, act, sound, and feel like when achieving success in your mind's eye. Regularly inhabit this space and explore all of the nuances that arise.
  - Visualize spaces, places, and faces that trigger an emotionally reactive response. Practice staying emotionally regulated in their presence by imagining it first.
  - Return to that upcoming high-pressure situation and utilize imagery to practice success.
  - Plan to make it realistic as possible, including the timing.

- SMART*AF* goals
  - Write the goals that you have in your career.
  - For each goal identify four or five alternatives that could be equally rewarding and fulfilling.
  - Make a plan to celebrate your success when you achieve a goal.
- Reward fulfillment
  - Create a lists of rewards that you can give to yourself for achieving your goals.
  - Add lots of little rewards:
    - A walk in the park
    - A nice stretch
    - A favorite beverage
  - A few moderate ones:
    - A night out
    - A day trip
  - Add one or two big ones:
    - Big ticket items
    - Extended time items
  - Return to this list and choose items to reward yourself with as you begin achieving your goals.
- Mindfulness[35]
  - Self-kindness vs. self-criticism
    - Embrace yourself for being warm and supportive, even when confronted with shortcomings.
  - Common humanity vs. isolation
    - Share mistakes and suffering as part of the human experience.
  - De-identification: Take a balanced view of yourself
    - Avoid rumination on, overidentification with, and dwelling in emotions.

Cultivate a Robust and Diverse Mentor Network[36]

It helps to have a core group of people that you can share thoughts and concern with, and gather strength, camaraderie, and good advice in return. Choosing people inside and outside of your professional environment adds hybrid vigor and psychological safety to discuss sensitive topics in appropriate arenas. In this sense, the community you build and sustain can help combat the isolation that often feeds imposter syndrome and limiting beliefs.

- Create discussions that provide the ability to "normalize struggle and failure."[37]
- Metabolize experiences through discussing them and processing them with this group.
- Create affinity groups that understand where you are coming from.
  - The people in these groups could share common characteristics with which you identify strongly:
    - Demographics
    - Expertise
    - Interests
- Build a community that can nurture you and support you.[38]
  - Create a list of mentors who you could reach out to.
  - Identify peers who offer great co-mentorship by being a supportive shoulder, listening ear, and good advice giver.
  - Identify people you could mentor and share your experience and personal story with them.

> **Pro Tip:** When working to change behavior rewards are important! You can reward yourself with a deep breath, a nice stretch, a refreshing beverage, a walk with fresh air, or something more personal.

Somatic Drills

Sometimes we forget that our body and mind are intimately connected. The somatic drills below help to ground you in the present moment and reduce the threat level that your nervous system might be experiencing. Access these drills when you notice limiting beliefs trapping you in cycles of negative thought.

- *4-7-8 breathing*
  - Blow out all your old air.
  - Breath in for four counts.
  - Suspend the breath for seven counts.
  - Breath out for eight counts.

- *Progressive muscle relaxation/body scan meditation*
  - Stand or sit in a comfortable position.
  - Allow the spine to lengthen and gather while noticing the tidal wave of your breath.
  - Beginning with the top of your head at the scalp, intentionally release any unnecessary muscle contraction.
  - Soften the forehead.
  - Calm the eyes.
  - Loosen the jaw.
  - Release the tongue.
  - Unwind the neck.
  - Thaw the shoulders.
  - Feel the width of the rib cage.
  - Ease the belly.
  - Find movement in the hips.
  - Release the knees away from the body.
  - Allow the heels to spread back and the toes to splay forward.

Notes

1 Korn Ferry, *Workforce 2024: Global Insights Report*, 2024, 30. https://www.kornferry.com/insights/featured-topics/workforce-management/workforce-planning-insights

2 Korn Ferry, *Workforce 2024: Global Insights Report*, 2024, 30. https://www.kornferry.com/insights/featured-topics/workforce-management/workforce-planning-insights

3 Kevin O. Cokley, ed., *The Impostor Phenomenon : Psychological Research, Theory, and Interventions* (Washington, DC: American Psychological Association, 2024), 312.

4 Korn Ferry, *Workforce 2024: Global Insights Report*, 2024, 30. https://www.kornferry.com/insights/featured-topics/workforce-management/workforce-planning-insights

5 Dena M. Bravata et al., "Prevalence, Predictors, and Treatment of Impostor Syndrome: A Systematic Review," *Journal of General Internal Medicine* 35, no. 4 (Apr, 2020), 1252–1275. https://doi.org/10.1007/s11606-019-05364-1

6 Kevin O. Cokley, ed., *The Impostor Phenomenon : Psychological Research, Theory, and Interventions* (Washington, DC: American Psychological Association, 2024), 309.

7 Kevin O. Cokley, ed., *The Impostor Phenomenon : Psychological Research, Theory, and Interventions* (Washington, DC: American Psychological Association, 2024).

8 Kevin O. Cokley, ed., *The Impostor Phenomenon : Psychological Research, Theory, and Interventions* (Washington, DC: American Psychological Association, 2024).

9 Kevin O. Cokley, ed., *The Impostor Phenomenon : Psychological Research, Theory, and Interventions* (Washington, DC: American Psychological Association, 2024), 311.

10 Brian R. Little, *Me, Myself and Us: The Science of Personality and the Art of Well-Being* (Canada: HarperCollins, 2015).

11 Melissa A. Lewis et al., "Applying Psychological Theories to Promote Long-Term Maintenance of Health Behaviors," *American Journal of Health Promotion* 30, no. 6 (2016): 381–394.

12 Kevin O. Cokley, ed., *The Impostor Phenomenon : Psychological Research, Theory, and Interventions* (Washington, DC: American Psychological Association, 2024), 311.

13 Andrea Calderone, Desirée Latella, Federica Impellizzeri, Paolo de Pasquale, Fausto Famà, Angelo Quartarone and R. S. Calabrò. "Neurobiological Changes Induced by Mindfulness and Meditation: A Systematic Review." *Biomedicines* 12 (2024). https://doi.org/10.3390/biomedicines12112613

14 Andrea Calderone, Desirée Latella, Federica Impellizzeri, Paolo de Pasquale, Fausto Famà, Angelo Quartarone and R. S. Calabrò. "Neurobiological Changes Induced by Mindfulness and Meditation: A Systematic Review." *Biomedicines* 12 (2024). https://doi.org/10.3390/biomedicines12112613

15 Stewart I. Donaldson and Matthew Dubin, *Flow 2.0: Optimal Experience in a Complex World. Honoring Mihaly Csikszentmihalyi's Legacy*, 1st ed. (Newark: John Wiley & Sons, Incorporated, 2024).

16 Matt Abrahams, *Think Fast, Talk Smarter: How to Speak Successfully When You're Put on the Spot* (New York: Simon Element, 2023).

17 Alison Wood Brooks, "Get Excited: Reappraising Pre-Performance Anxiety as Excitement," *Journal of Experimental Psychology: General* 143, no. 3 (2014), 1144–1158. https://doi.org/10.1037/a0035325

18 Alison Wood Brooks, "Get Excited: Reappraising Pre-Performance Anxiety as Excitement," *Journal of Experimental Psychology: General* 143, no. 3 (2014), 1154. https://doi.org/10.1037/a0035325

19 Ronald E. Smith and James C. Ascough, *Promoting Emotional Resilience: Cognitive-Affective Stress Management Training* (New York, NY: The Guilford Press, 2016).

20 Ronald E. Smith and James C. Ascough, *Promoting Emotional Resilience: Cognitive-Affective Stress Management Training* (New York, NY: The Guilford Press, 2016).

21 Ronald E. Smith and James C. Ascough, *Promoting Emotional Resilience: Cognitive-Affective Stress Management Training* (New York, NY: The Guilford Press, 2016).

22 David Tod and Martin Eubank, eds., *Applied Sport, Exercise, and Performance Psychology Current Approaches to Helping Clients* (London: Routledge, 2020).

23 Kate F. Hays, ed., *Performance Psychology in Action : A Casebook for Working with Athletes, Performing Artists, Business Leaders, and Professionals in High-Risk Occupations*, 1st ed. (Washington, DC: American Psychological Association, 2009).

24 Melissa Romano, *Vagus Nerve Deck* (New York, NY: Zeitgeist, 2024).

25 Alexander T. Latinjak et al., "Self-Talk: An Interdisciplinary Review and Transdisciplinary Model," *Review of General Psychology* 27, no. 4 (2023), 373. https://doi.org/10.1177/10892680231170263

26 Richard F. Gerson, *The Executive Athlete : How Sport Psychology Helps Business People Become World-Class Performers*, 1st ed. (Amherst, Mass: HRD Press, 2008), Chap. 6.

27 Kate F. Hays, ed., *Performance Psychology in Action : A Casebook for Working with Athletes, Performing Artists, Business Leaders, and Professionals in*

High-Risk Occupations, 1st ed. (Washington, DC: American Psychological Association, 2009).

28 N. Ashraf et al., "Learning to See the World's Opportunities: The Impact of Imagery on Entrepreneurial Success," (2022). https://consensus.app/papers/learning-to-see-the-world-%E2%80%99-s-opportunities-the-impact-of-ashraf-bryan/89873285700353c48a393f43a03120bb/

29 Hays, ed., *Performance Psychology in Action : A Casebook for Working with Athletes, Performing Artists, Business Leaders, and Professionals in High-Risk Occupations*, 1st ed. (Washington, DC: American Psychological Association, 2009), 15.

30 Stewart I. Donaldson and Matthew Dubin, *Flow 2.0: Optimal Experience in a Complex World. Honoring Mihaly Csikszentmihalyi's Legacy*, 1st ed. (Newark: John Wiley & Sons, Incorporated, 2024), 13.

31 Stewart I. Donaldson and Matthew Dubin, *Flow 2.0: Optimal Experience in a Complex World. Honoring Mihaly Csikszentmihalyi's Legacy*, 1st ed. (Newark: John Wiley & Sons, Incorporated, 2024), 11.

32 Stewart I. Donaldson and Matthew Dubin, *Flow 2.0: Optimal Experience in a Complex World. Honoring Mihaly Csikszentmihalyi's Legacy*, 1st ed. (Newark: John Wiley & Sons, Incorporated, 2024), 11.

33 Ellen P. Lukens and William R. McFarlane, "Psychoeducation as Evidence-Based Practice: Considerations for Practice, Research, and Policy," *Brief Treatment and Crisis Intervention* 4, no. 3 (2004): 205–225, https://doi.org/10.1093/brief-treatment/mhh019

34 Kevin O. Cokley, ed., *The Impostor Phenomenon : Psychological Research, Theory, and Interventions* (Washington, DC: American Psychological Association, 2024), 316.

35 Kevin O. Cokley, ed., *The Impostor Phenomenon : Psychological Research, Theory, and Interventions* (Washington, DC: American Psychological Association, 2024), 316.

36 Mae Manongsong Ague and Rajashi Ghosh, "Developing the Positive Identity of Minoritized Women Leaders in Higher Education: How Can Multiple and Diverse Developers Help with Overcoming the Impostor Phenomenon?" *Human Resource Development Review* 20, no. 4 (2021), 436–485. https://doi.org/10.1177/15344843211040732

37 Kevin O. Cokley, ed., *The Impostor Phenomenon : Psychological Research, Theory, and Interventions* (Washington, DC: American Psychological Association, 2024), 321.

38 Mae Manongsong Ague and Rajashi Ghosh, "Developing the Positive Identity of Minoritized Women Leaders in Higher Education: How Can Multiple and Diverse Developers Help with Overcoming the Impostor Phenomenon?" *Human Resource Development Review* 20, no. 4 (2021), 436–485. https://doi.org/10.1177/15344843211040732

Section III

Skills Building

Chapter 7

Body Language and Virtual Communication

Inform—Why It Matters

When the eyes and ears compete, the eyes win. An estimated 68–93% of a message's meaning is nonverbal. As stated by Subrat Kumar and Sundar Ray, those who display executive presence have an "ability to command a room, connect with their audience on a deeper level, and convey their vision with clarity and conviction ... [and] nonverbal cues are the silent yet powerful signals."[1] Once again, it's not just what you say but how you say it. Through nonverbal communication, we convey our level of comfort, interpersonal engagement, emotion, authenticity, and confidence.

Whenever you are present with another, whether in person, on the phone, or virtually, you cannot *not* communicate. As soon as someone enters the space, we notice their posture, movement, appearance, facial display, gestures, and use of time. As soon as someone speaks, vocal aspects including volume, vocal variety, pace, pitch, and articulation create perceptions that either enhance or detract from their message. Your audience, whether one or many, is attuned to the messages you are sending both verbally and nonverbally.

Powerful nonverbal cues do not always include cues of dominance or extroversion. They can also convey composure, a sense of self, and quiet dignity. Elements of nonverbal communication related to executive presence include appearance, self-confidence, and engagement skills.

Understanding nonverbal communication benefits you in two ways:

1 It allows you to adopt behaviors that:

   a Enhance executive presence
   b Increase personal confidence
   c Enhance message reception

DOI: 10.4324/9781003624950-10

2   It enables you to read what others are conveying nonverbally and:

 a   Increase awareness of their emotional state
 b   Improve interpersonal dynamics
 c   Adapt your delivery to achieve situational goals

Body language expert Dr. Amy Cuddy of Harvard University conducted several studies on how body language not only affects *how others perceive us* but also how we *feel about ourselves*. We can change our neurochemistry by displaying certain body language. In her studies, participants were asked to sit or stand in either "confident" or "weak" positions for two minutes. Their hormone levels were measured both before and after assuming the assigned postures. The study found that those who assumed confident positions experienced a rise in testosterone, the hormone associated with confidence. Those assuming weak positions had a rise in cortisol levels, the hormone associated with stress. The study concluded that not only does our body language send a message to others but directly affects our physiological and mental state. In her 2012 TED Talk, *Your Body Language May Shape Who You Are*, she famously told the audience, "Don't fake it till you make it. Fake it until you become it."[2]

Equip—Skills or Behaviors That Enhance the Area in Focus

Let's break down nonverbal communication beginning with aspects of body language and how they affect our perceptions and feelings of confidence, engagement, and sincerity.

Posture

Posture refers to how you hold yourself and includes spinal alignment, shoulders, and head position.

When standing, having a grounded stance with feet apart and hips in line with shoulders conveys strength. Crossing your feet can lead to leaning or swaying, which can be distracting and convey discomfort or insecurity.

When seated, there are two possibilities for appearing confident. To adopt a confident and engaged posture, sit forward and tall, head tilted up, taking up space by hand placement or gestures. For a confident-yet-relaxed posture, sit back, head tilted upward, and spread out. This is conveyed mostly in social situations or where you feel comfortable engaging in a more laid-back approach to conversation or interaction.

Figure 7.1 Good posture standing

Figure 7.2 Confident but relaxed seated position

Walking with Purpose

Impostor syndrome is real. Remember, it is normal to be somewhat insecure when walking into a new or high-pressure space. Before entering a room, engage in positive self-talk. You deserve to be there, so "own the space." Those who display confidence walk with purpose and ease.

We each have a natural gate. It is not about changing how you walk, but by employing these four simple behaviors:

1 Think tall.
2 Pull shoulders back.
3 Keep eyes forward. Look toward your destination and acknowledge individuals in the room.
4 Keep gestures loose, with your arms free to swing or move.

To see examples, watch the YouTube video "Confidence" by Joe Navarro, a former FBI agent and body language expert. In the first few minutes you will see politicians, athletes, actors, and singers enter a room or cross a space with purpose and ease. Navarro breaks down their entrances, movements, and use of time.

Facial Display

Facial display includes eye contact, smiles, frowns, and eyebrow movement. These movements add meaning to our messages and increase engagement with our audience.

Our eyes provide insight into our emotional state. "Eye gaze is a potent source of social information with direct eye gaze signaling the desire to approach and averted eye gaze signaling avoidance."[3] Research has shown that a speaker who makes and holds eye contact is perceived as having increased levels of:

• Sophistication .
• Competence
• Intelligence

The key is to convey that you can look someone in the eye to establish connection and engagement. Do not feel as if you need to hold eye contact with someone for an uncomfortable amount of time. Think of eye contact like a handshake. Create a strong connection at the beginning, then as the conversation continues feel free to look away as you listen from time to time and reestablish eye contact occasionally. Think of it as an act of paying attention to others by acknowledging their presence.

When presenting to a group, one method of establishing eye contact and diffusing anxiety is to find three friendly faces. To do this, enter the space (virtual or in-person) early and engage in conversation or introduce yourself to several people. This breaks the social distance barrier and helps you to identify individuals who will respond with positive nonverbals when you look out at them. As the meeting or presentation continues, you can let your gaze to fall on an increasing number of participants.

Smiling is a universal sign of happiness, pleasure, and enthusiasm. Smiling, like other nonverbal behaviors, affects our audience's interpretation of the message and interaction as well as our own emotions. Research shows that "there are both physiological and psychological benefits from maintaining positive facial expressions during stress."[4]

Smiling has a ripple effect on our eyes and voice. Smiling also lifts the mouth palette and brightens the tone of your voice. This is the reason salespeople are trained to smile when speaking on the phone. A genuine smile reaches the eyes, and studies show that people can easily distinguish between a fake and sincere smile.

When presenting, we often forget our face. A speaker can become so focused on conveying the verbal information correctly, that they forget to convey enthusiasm for the topic through facial display. Don't forget to smile!

What to do:

- Show enthusiasm for your message through facial display.
- Make eye contact with one person for one idea. Allow your eyes to fall on different people around the room throughout the message.
- Record yourself when practicing or delivering a presentation. View the recording to pay specific attention to facial display and level of dynamism.

Hand Gestures

The use of our hands, arms, and head movement confirms or contradicts our verbal messages. Based on the use of gestures, we are seen as either warm, energetic, and agreeable or cold, distant, and insecure.

People favor leaders who use an increased number and variety of hand gestures. Purposive, planned, movements that visually represent what we are saying are beneficial for audience interpretation. If you are opening with "There are three main goals of the project," gesture the number three by holding up three fingers. This does two things: It conveys confidence, and it plants the number three in conjunction with your main points in the audience's long-term memory.

Constant or aimless movement like fidgeting with a pen, jewelry, or hair, indicates nervousness. Self-touch gestures like rubbing your hands, touching your neck or face indicate a feeling of uneasiness or insecurity. Often, we are unaware of displaying such gestures. This is why recording yourself giving a presentation or leading a meeting is beneficial for self-awareness and regulation.

> **Pro Tip:** Create a long-term memory of your verbal message by visually representing it through body language and gestures. Example: If you say "three", show three.

Gesture Dos and Don'ts

When using your hands while speaking, two gestures to avoid are the "stop" and "down" hand movements. The "stop" gesture signals resistance and pushing away from your audience. The "down" gesture has negative connotations unless you are saying "bring it down" or "slow down."

Figure 7.3 Hands in "stop" gesture   *Figure 7.4* Hands in "down" gesture

Figure 7.5 Hands in "open" gesture

Figure 7.6 Hands in "steeple"

More positive body language includes "palm up" gestures and the "steeple" position. When speaking, palm up hand gestures signal openness and transparency. You may use this gesture with one or both hands while speaking.

One great tool to adopt is the "steeple." The "steeple" gives you a confident resting-hands position. When you don't know what to do with your hands, place your hands together in front of your mid-section with your fingers gently touching. This is a solid place to come back to between gesturing. Why is it a positive gesture? It demonstrates a composed and more controlled sense of movement.

Using your hands while speaking is natural. Don't try to over-regulate your gestures. Authentic, natural gestures come across as engaging and conversational. Just be aware of using more open and measured gestures.

Table 7.1 The Dos and Don'ts of Gestures

Do	Don't
Steeple	Cross arms or hands behind back
Palms open and up	Palms gesturing down or stop
Point with whole hand	Point with extended finger

Frame for Gestures

Let's draw a box around an area of natural hand movement.

Standing In-Person Communication

Stand and put your fingers in front of your breastbone. Now draw a box that extends from your shoulders, down to out beside your hips, and now back in under your belly button. This is your hand gesture box when face-to-face. Hand or arm movements outside of this box need to intentionally indicate grandiosity.

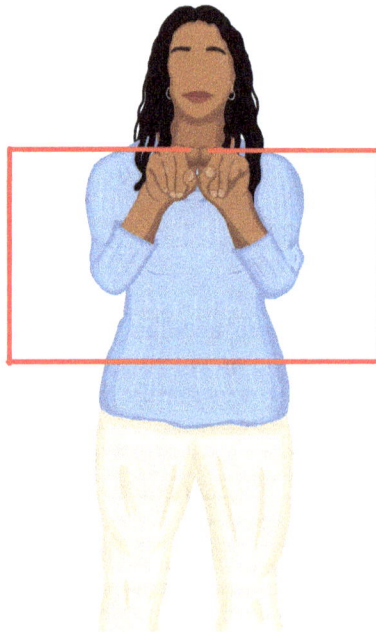

Figure 7.7 Box for hand gestures when standing

Seated In-Person or Virtual Communication

To create the seated gesture box, start with fingers together under your chin. Move them out minimally past your shoulders, down to chest level, and back to breastbone. We've simply raised and narrowed the gesture box. Showing hand gestures within the frame as we speak is powerful. By showing gestures within the frame, you communicate more engagement, transparency, and confidence.

One last tip. This subtle gesture indicates that you are tuned in to the speaker while also reminding you to be an effective listener. When someone is speaking, slightly shift your head to show the person your ear.

This is a gentle gesture. Don't go overboard. If you have longer hair, simply tuck your hair behind your ear and gesture that you are listening. You will be amazed at how this minor gesture can communicate that you are engaged and interested and value their message.

Figure 7.8 Box for hand gestures when seated

Figure 7.9 Attentive ear gesture

Virtual Presence

How are you "showing up" virtually? Think of a professional you've experienced who has appeared on camera in a manner that was less than professional manner. Were they cast in darkness? Sitting too far away from the camera? Looking sideways at another monitor? How we show up virtually matters just as much as how we show up in person. Here are three strategies for enhancing your executive presence on camera.

Set the Stage

While communicating virtually, we are in a box. This is a window into our space. Our background gives the audience a sense of who we are and our level of professionalism.

Space, more formally called proxemics, is considered nonverbal communication. It is the arrangement of semi-fixed objects like furniture, art, etc. We have all seen someone joining a meeting from their car or bedroom. What someone shows us of their physical space or background impacts how we view their professionalism and status as a leader.

Take a moment to think about the impressions you are attempting to make. Could your background help you to create some of those impressions? Whether you are in an office with a bookshelf behind you, in front of a solid painted wall—dark walls create wonderful contrast and a clean look—or have a high-quality virtual image, your background sets the stage.

Picture Perfect

Lighting is vital. The goal is to have a light source in front of you, not behind you. Light coming from behind casts you in darkness. This lack of light prevents your audience from seeing your face, missing out on your nonverbal cues.

If possible, situate yourself across from a window to allow the light to fall upon your face. If a natural light source is not available, position a lamp in front of your computer or a ring light that hooks onto the top. Ceiling lights, especially fluorescent lights with white-blue hues, create a harsh look shining down on you from above. When possible, utilize natural or soft light options.

Positioning

How close to the camera should you sit or stand? How should you angle your camera? These are considerations of framing.

You want your camera to be at eye level. One professional tip is to use an external camera that plugs in and sits at the top of your monitor. When engaging with one person in a virtual meeting, place the "view" on

Table 7.2 The Do's and Don'ts of Setting the Stage Virtually

Do	Don't
Face a warm or natural source of light	Have a window or light behind you
Sit close enough to signal engagement	Sit far away from camera
Have camera at eye level	Have camera beneath face (looking up your nose)

"speaker view". This keeps you looking directly ahead rather than to one side and eliminates the distraction of focusing on yourself.

Adjust to sit close enough to fill the frame. Check to see how you look on your screen and make sure you have created some space above your head. Move in close enough that your audience sees your shoulders and upper arms. Position your camera so that you are looking straight ahead and at eye-level as if you were standing face-to-face with your audience.

For those of you who use two monitors, be mindful of looking away and to the side. You may be engaged, but your audience sees it as distracted and multitasking.

Pro Tip: Prior to attending a virtual meeting, go to the site you most commonly use (Zoom, Teams, etc.) and start a private session. This allows you to see how you will appear on camera, your lighting, and background. Make any adjustments needed before joining the scheduled meeting.

Figure 7.10 Person framed well within virtual "box"

The Power of Silence

Silence is a nonverbal cue. It creates space and provides a break from speaking that brings attention back to you, the speaker. It shows a self-assured command of time that conveys a sense of calmness, confidence, and knowledge. Time is the temporal aspect of nonverbal communication. Temporal, as in tempo.

Studies have shown that people who vary their speaking tempo and embrace a slower pace command more attention. Additionally, to plan pauses before speaking and breaks within speech is a tool of oration used by some of the most effective speakers and leaders. Silence is indeed golden.

Silence allows people's attention to fall on you or to bring the attention back. When you are speaking, as in a presentation, your constant vocalizing becomes white-noise. Strategic pauses create tension through brief silence which piques the interest of the audience, attuning their ears back to your message. Great speakers throughout time have used strategic pauses and silences to great effect. Churchill was known to write pauses into his speeches along with the length of each pause.

Silence can be scary. It places you in the spotlight. Part of executive presence is becoming comfortable taking up space. *One way to do this is to count to three in your head, slowly.* This may seem like an eternity to you but to an audience, it is just a momentary break in the noise that recalibrates their ears and allows their attention to fall back to the speaker.

Three tips for using time and silence effectively:

1   When you walk to the front of the room or stand to begin a meeting or presentation, find your position and count to three slowly in your head before speaking the first word.
2   When introducing new information or a complex idea, state it, pause, then repeat. The pause allows the information to sink in and repeating it increases retention and understanding of the information by your audience.
3   When asked a question, raise your eyebrows and count to three slowly before replying. This indicates interest and thoughtfulness. Show interest in the question and give a thoughtful rather than a reactive response.

To view a demonstration of the power of silence, watch former FBI agent Joe Navarro's YouTube video on *Confidence*. He shows video clips of former Secretary of State Colin Powell, former Chancellor of Germany

Angela Merkel, Martin Luther King, and Churchill utilizing timing and silence as nonverbal indicators of power.

> **Pro Tip:** Use pausing and silence as a de-escalation technique. Leaders who are seen as confident display "grace under fire" and "self-composure" in stress-filled situations and crucial conversations. Pause, breathe, and take a beat (count to three) before responding.

Cultural Considerations

This chapter is written with a Western cultural perspective on body language. Various cultures portray and perceive nonverbal communication differently. Some brief examples include:

- Eye contact: In Western cultures, direct eye contact is often perceived as a sign of confidence and honesty. In Asian cultures, prolonged eye contact might be seen as confrontational or disrespectful.
- Personal space: North Americans and Europeans generally value personal space, while individuals from Latin American or Middle Eastern cultures may prefer closer proximity during conversations.
- Communication style: High-context cultures (e.g., Japan, Saudi Arabia) rely heavily on nonverbal cues and context for communication. Low-context cultures (e.g., the United States, Germany) prioritize direct and explicit communication.

Understanding the body language and nonverbal communication of others helps you to give insight into their level of engagement, understanding, or emotional response. Interculturally, become aware of potential variations in nonverbal communication and adapt where possible. Understanding these nuances can improve interactions and prevent misinterpretations in multicultural settings.

Activate—Try It on!

Those who display executive presence are aware of their body language. The goal is to convey self-confidence and composure through our nonverbal communication. Activation begins with an honest inventory of how you are currently showing up and identifying the behaviors that would elevate your presence.

Body Language Audit

Over the next week, take stock of how you move, sit, and interact currently in the following *in-person* situations:

1 In a meeting: How are you sitting? Are you displaying confidence and engagement, or insecurity and discomfort? Are you taking up space physically, sitting tall with arms relaxed and open, using hand gestures when speaking? What nonverbal behaviors might you adopt to create the feeling and perception of greater ease and confidence?
2 In a one-on-one conversation: Do you establish eye contact at the beginning of the conversation? Are you enhancing your message using facial display as you speak? Are you giving nonverbal feedback while the other person is speaking? Are you actively listening and signaling that you are tuned in? What area of interpersonal interaction could you improve through body language?
3 Speaking to a group: Are you engaged and making eye contact and facial expressions that enhance your message? Are you gesturing with open and inviting movements? What nonverbal behaviors will you become more aware of and "try on" for your next speaking opportunity?
4 Virtually: How are you "showing up"? Are you taking advantage of being able to set the stage to convey credibility? What aspects of body language are in need of improvement? List two or three actions you will take to show up more confidently during your next virtual encounter.

Notes

1 Subrat Kumar Sundar Ray, "Executive Presence: Elevating Your Leadership and Career," *The ICFAI Journal of Soft Skills* 18, no. 1 (2024): 29–33.
2 Amy Cuddy, *Your Body Language May Shape Who You Are*, TED Talk, filmed June 2012 at TEDGlobal, posted October 2012, https://www.ted.com/talks/amy_cuddy_your_body_language_may_shape_who_you_are
3 Saara Khalid, Jason C. Deska, and Kurt Hugenberg, "The Eyes Are the Windows to the Mind: Direct Eye Gaze Triggers the Ascription of Others' Minds," *Personality and Social Psychology Bulletin* 42, no. 12 (2016): 1666–1677.
4 Tara L. Kraft and Sarah D. Pressman, "Grin and Bear It: The Influence of Manipulated Facial Expression on the Stress Response," *Psychological Science* 23, no. 11 (2012): 1372–1378.

Chapter 8

Finding Your Voice

Inform—Why It Matters

During the average day, your vocal folds collide over one million times and travel over 5,000 meters.[1] That is a mini-marathon for a small group of muscles, the average diameter of which is between a dime and a nickel in diameter. Such an extensive use of vocal folds comes with its risks. Nearly 21% of those surveyed reported experiencing a voice disorder, characterized by difficulty speaking, at some point in their lives.[2] Significantly, this same study identified the use of voice-assistant technology (think of asking Siri to tell you the forecast) and teleconferencing as emerging risk factors for our voices, as they alter the typical patterns we use when speaking.[3]

However, that is just your *outer voice*, the one you use to communicate with other people or devices. You also possess the ability to speak, philosophize, and even debate using your *inner voice*, the one you hear right now as you are reading these words. The inner voice is involved in "planning, problem-solving, self-motivating, reading, writing, calculating, and autobiographical memory."[4] These represent some of the key tasks in cultivating executive presence, and you spend approximately 25% of your waking hours using this internal type of speech.[5]

Whether it is the inner voice or the outer voice, your voice carries a significant responsibility and has a profound impact. This is especially true for those in leadership positions or aspiring to them. But, sometimes it is hard to have confidence in our voice, and rarely do we take dedicated time to focus on training our voice for speech. Sometimes, it's even hard to feel your voice as an embodied part of yourself; it can evaporate into thin air and become brittle, tight, shaky, or unreliable when you're nervous. Since the nervous and respiratory systems directly influence your voice, it is affected by every beat of your heart. Despite this, when we are trying to communicate confidence, build consensus, or motivate teams, our voices bear the brunt of the work. This has a

DOI: 10.4324/9781003624950-11

substantial impact on your executive presence and your success. To enhance both, it is necessary to become more clear on the role the body and mind play in finding your voice.

Mind the Tone

A groundbreaking 2002 study found that when listeners judged surgeons' voices as sounding too dominant and not concerned enough, those same surgeons were almost twice as likely to be sued for malpractice than those whose vocal tone and demeanor were judged to be less dominant and more concerned.[6] In this study, audio clips of 65 surgeons were recorded in 114 conversations with patients during routine medical visits. They were filtered so that only the expressive features remained: intonation, speed, pitch, and rhythm. The clips were then anonymized and rated on a seven-point scale, ranging from "not at all" to "extremely," by a group of Harvard University undergraduates using the following descriptors: Warm, anxious/concerned, interested, hostile, sympathetic, professional, competent, dominant, satisfied, and genuine. The results indicated that after listening to just 40 seconds of a surgeon's speech, with all other identifiers withheld, the ratings could accurately predict which surgeons had been sued.[7] These results held across multiple surgical disciplines. This was the first study to demonstrate clear associations between communication and malpractice in surgeons; however, subsequent years of research have supported this finding. The expressive features in the way we use our voice impact those who are listening to us and how they feel about our interactions after we've gone.

The Outer Voice

Most texts on executive presence discuss how to use the voice obliquely, but we will delve into the anatomical, physiological, mental, and technical considerations. This is because they rest on the four common misconceptions that often hold people back from unlocking the full potential of their voice.

I Have a Strong, Weak, Nasal, or Good Voice

Your voice is not a fixed concept, figuratively or physiologically. The larynx, which houses the vocal folds, is suspended from the hyoid bone, the only bone in the body not attached to another bone, so it has a remarkable amount of mobility. It is an amazingly versatile instrument in form and function. Place a finger on the front of your neck and swallow to feel just how mobile it is. Anatomical and physiological changes in our larynx begin before birth and never stop completely as we age.[8] Although the structure is determined through genetics and hormones, culture influences physiology—we develop musculature associated with the languages we learn to speak as children.

When linked to the incredible resource that is the human imagination, the possibilities for phonation are quite literally endless—so too are the sounds that we can make. Just think of all the words that humans have created across the 7,000 modern spoken languages of the world.[9] Most babies arrive on the planet with the software to download any of those languages.

Now consider all the sounds humans create for paralanguage or nonlinguistic communication:

- What is the sound you make when you smell fresh, warm bread?
- What do you say when you see a litter of puppies?
- Now, think of the sound you make when someone steps on your foot.

These sounds are incredibly expressive and communicative without much practice. They also change in quality and volume to fit the circumstance rather than being stuck in one affect. Through training, our voices can regularly access the full spectrum of expressive features, making a more positive impression.

Instead of thinking you *have* a certain type of voice, imagine that you are *accessing* a particular type of voice use for the occasion. This bit of flexibility can free you up to vary your vocal approach to meet the moment.

The Sound of My Voice Just Isn't That Important

The second misconception involves how we perceive, or more accurately, how we hear ourselves. Most people don't consider themselves professional voice users and consequently don't realize the significant impact it has on their executive presence. However, experts say that an occupational or professional voice user is anyone whose voice is essential to their job and who relies on it for their employability.[10] In other words, if you need to use your voice to get hired or do your job, and doing your job without it would be more difficult, you are a professional voice user. Your executive presence benefits from treating the voice as an instrument to be tuned, maintained, and cared for rather than an afterthought.

I Think about My Voice When It Matters

The third misconception involves giving attention to the voice only for the big moments. Those would be the planned speeches or presentations where you are in front of the room. Day-to-day interactions are just as integral, and perhaps more influential, in shaping how others perceive you. Do you remember when many meetings suddenly switched from in-person to on-line during the pandemic? Voices took on a greater share of the communication work because there was no longer such a reliance on body language and gestures. We inferred a great deal about our colleagues from the tone of their voice and the tempo of their speech. This still happens even when we are face-to-face. A great deal of information is encoded into the tone when we speak. To manage impressions over time, your voice matters in every interaction.

I don't Talk at Work

The last misconception is that if you don't speak a lot or don't need to speak, the voice isn't important. Your voice is a part of your work, even if you aren't talking to another person. Your inner voice, the one you're using while reading this right now, can either contribute to or detract from your well-being. Whether you are reading something or listening to someone, the voice remains active.[11] You can either direct it or be directed by it.

Primal Sound Improves Efficiency

Now that we've considered all the reasons why paying attention to our voices is important, let's explore an intuitive approach to discovering your authentic voice. As a starting point, we need to consider the nature of sound. It's important to remember that sound does not naturally project in a focused beam like light. Instead, sound waves radiate in all directions. What we perceive as a great speaking voice is the resonance of the vocal tract being naturally amplified. That resonance is a passive process.[12] Since resonance is a passive process, effort does not increase the quality, tone, range, or reach of the voice. It can have the opposite effect. Efficiency, however, does. We approach efficient vocal production when the least amount of muscular contraction yields the most amount of reverberation.

It's helpful here to think of a great singer, one that always makes the most difficult notes look relatively easy or even fun. You can develop a resonance strategy that allows the articulators (tongue and throat) to aid in the amplification of the sound emanating from the source (larynx), and the good news is that you already have a head start.

What is the first thing we do when we enter this world? We cry! We produce a sound that fills ears, hearts, and hallways, immediately evoking a response from those around us. Exclamations of joy, surprise, pain, or agony rarely need external amplification or much thought to them at all. In response to these impulses, our instinct kicks in. You have probably never spent an evening laughing with friends and been vocally tired the next day from the laughter. You probably also filled the room, and if the laughter carried on late into the night, you worried about being too loud rather than the opposite. It is hard to keep the decibels from piling up in these situations. What if you could harness that feeling when it was time to deliver an important speech with all eyes on you? That same breath and resonance strategy can be highly effective when training the speaking voice to exhibit the qualities of audibility and confidence associated with executive presence. Our body already contains this knowledge.

You don't need to cry like a baby to exhibit executive presence. Still, you can adopt a similar strategy to ensure your coordination is efficient and you are recruiting the optimal muscle groups. The advice in the Equip section and the exercises in the Activate section help to make the connection between this innate ability and the unnatural situation of speaking in front of large groups in high-pressure situations. Your primal sound is the key to harnessing a type of coordination in your body that you already know but might need help connecting to professional applications.

Equip—Skills or Behaviors That Enhance the Area in Focus

The Inner Voice

The fact that we have a voice that is tied exclusively to our imagination gives you a hint of its power. Also referred to as the *covert* voice, as opposed to the *overt* voice, it helps you process abstract concepts and memories while making sense of a confusing world.[13] The inner voice is primarily responsible for task-switching and problem-solving. When tapping into the inner voice, you are using a similar neural network to the one you use for the outer voice. This is significant because what we practice we perfect. If you want to make a lasting impact with your voice, you must start with the inner one, imagining efficient coordination even when you aren't speaking out loud.

Without direction and cultivation, however, this voice can become cluttered with words, sounds, and negative ideas from others. Uninterrogated, it can become a terror. "It is hard to prevent oneself from generating verbal thoughts."[14] Being so closely tied to memory, the inner voice can easily replicate the hurtful, mean, or insulting things that have been said to us or projected onto us. It may even be challenging to separate yourself from those ideas and attribute them to an outside source after you have internalized them. The imagined voice has a big influence on our mood and how we see ourselves.

This means training your speech inside your head to have the rhythm and intonation that communicates your values through your message can add a tangible benefit to your quality of life. Many of the world's cultural traditions harness this powerful form of presence through internalized prayer or meditation. The mantras and texts associated with this type of mental concentration serve as a method of directing the inner voice to become a source of calm that can be utilized in demanding situations. You can borrow that pacing to keep your mind from racing.

Since the inner voice likes to solve problems, you can leverage this ability as well.[15] When you notice that particular train of thought has become destructive, pause and take a breath. Since this is an imagined voice, you can also imagine a different way forward. Select a problem or topic that requires your attention and direct your inner voice to it instead. It is excellent if you can keep the inner voice on this task, but it is also fine if the voice starts to wander into uncharted territory since mind-wandering is a useful skill. Psychologist and professor Richard Baars argues that "mind wandering, even if it appears irrelevant, unwanted, or intrusive, may still play an important adaptive role in life-relevant problem-solving and learning."[16] Allowing the mind to wander and even planning for it is a generous gift to yourself. Not only our body and mind but also our values and vision connect through the voice.

Primal Sound Primer

1 Make the sound of an irritated infant: "Mwahnh mwahnh mwahnh!"
2 Gradually transform the cries into the phrase, "Hi, how are you?"
3 Go back and forth between the two phrases a couple of times.
4 Follow this same process with laughing and giggling.

Reflect: Notice the energy, engagement, and coordination required to generate that sound. It might even feel a bit silly if you're not used to speaking that way. Laughing, giggling, and crying are wonderful primal sounds that act as quick voice lessons for the body.

These instinctual phonations:

1 Utilize the elastic recoil of the diaphragm and intercostal muscles.
2 Lower the larynx in a protective maneuver.
3 Optimize the pharynx by widening and spreading the soft palette.

As an evolutionary phenomenon, such sounds also serve as primal tools for connection. Professionals who struggle to make themselves heard when speaking often notice a dramatic resonance boost when they make those transfers between primal sound and public speaking. It's a way your body already knows to get good results. They can also serve as quick warm-ups.

Warm-ups Improve Flow Phonation

Warm-ups are an essential part of any athlete's routine. You see the most highly skilled professionals ensure adequate blood flow before heading onto the field so they can meet the moment with ease. The research suggests that warm-ups increase body temperature, stimulate the neuromuscular system, and prepare muscles to execute a desired task.[17] Actors and singers almost always include a warm-up routine before taking the stage. However, most professional speakers don't intentionally utilize this tool enough to make a significant impact and achieve good results. Since the voice rests in the mutable region of the body, an ideal warm-up considers the entire instrument to align all the parts. Refer to the semi-occluded vocal track exercises for more warm-up activities.

Body

There is a natural grace, elegance, and ease of a body that is well-aligned with itself. We notice it visually and also perceive it aurally. It is a core part of presence. It demonstrates that we are here, active, and aware of the moment we are in, rather than straining into the future or holding on to the past.

Six anatomical points of balance can enhance the body's flexibility and help achieve a resonant voice. In this sense, it is more helpful to think of balance rather than posture because micromovements and shifts are necessary to avoid excess muscular tension. Like an accordion, the staggered nature of the six places of balance allows the speaker to remain responsive and reflexive, whether seated or standing. It embodies the agility one needs as a leader.

Those places are

Heels
Knees
Hips
Lower back
Shoulders
Atlanto-occipital joint (at the base of the skull)

After quieting the mind, explore what level of tension you are holding at each location.

Breath

While experimenting with balance, you will notice that the primary action that moves the body is the breath. It sustains us in the present and in presence. Since the voice is a function of the respiratory system, how we

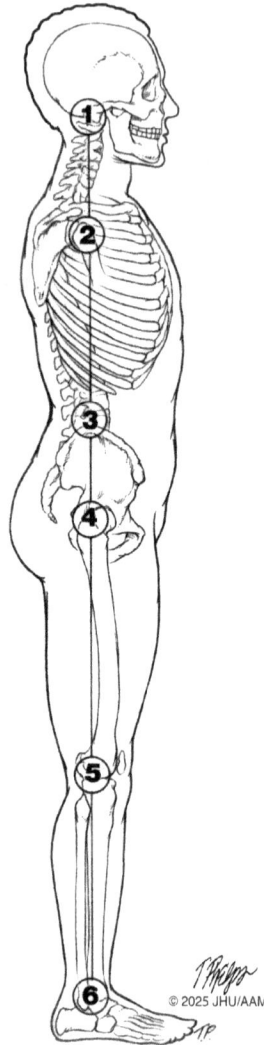

Figure 8.1 Six places of balance

conceptualize the breath has a substantial impact on the sound that we create. Each joint of the body responds to the breath, so we can optimize it by being receptive to movement. The breath typically functions at the subconscious level through the autonomic nervous system. Our breathing shifts in response to our needs and perceived threats, whether real or imagined. While this can prepare us for fight, flight, freeze, or fawn, presence demands that we demonstrate ease in high-stress situations, accessing the full range of motion available to us. Techniques that bring breath movement under the mindful guidance of awareness can calm the vagus nerve and restore feelings of calm.

Vocal Variety

The most important technical thing to remind yourself about the voice is that the larynx is suspended. This means it is natural to feel the larynx move up and down, and we want the space above it, the pharynx, to stay relatively open to get the best sound. Since the anatomical structures that produce the voice are hard to see, take a look at the anatomical sketch in Figure 8.2 and the megaphone in Figure 8.3. Notice the similarities in shape between the two figures.

When working well, the well-lubricated vocal folds glide and slide between their different functionalities with the feeling of an open throat. The voice community is not entirely in agreement on what to call these functionalities or registers, but for simplicity's sake, let's use the familiar names of *head voice* and *chest voice*. Using these terms is helpful because they direct you to where you are likely to feel the most sympathetic vibration. You can even lay one hand on your chest and the other on your forehead to build awareness of the difference between the two. With your lips gently closed for

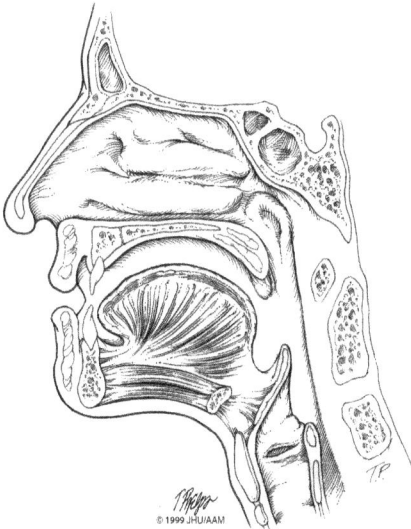

Figure 8.2 Sagittal plane of head

Figure 8.3 Megaphone

a hum, slowly ascend and descend in pitch over the entire compass of your range. It is likely two octaves or more are available to you in some form. Sensing those vibrations is helpful when considering finding your authentic voice—it serves as a feedback tool that lets you know you are speaking well.

Rarely do we need to use the entire range when speaking, but perhaps accessing a wider swath of it could catch the listener's ear. We have all listened to a speech where the speaker might have had interesting information to share, yet, the delivery was so monotone, speaking on one pitch or vibratory frequency, that it became almost impossible to stay focused. This *droning* seems to be a common response when high-pressure situations require intense focus and concentration. We might even consider it our "serious" voice to help us convey important information, although it comes across as uninteresting.

This type of voice use is unlikely to motivate, inspire, or even interest. Instead, *intoning* is the use of a broader range of pitches when speaking. Think of a roller coaster. If the track stayed flat the whole time, it wouldn't be nearly as much fun as a ride that had lots of changes in height. Or you could even imagine a song with only one note. Think of your favorite song, and just sing all of the lyrics on one note. Is it still your favorite song? Much of the information we transmit when speaking isn't in the words we say; it's how we say it. Studies have proved that we intuit attractiveness, leadership ability, intellect, and more to a speaker based on how they speak.[18]

Examples of Poor Voice Use

The following are examples of speech behavior that are often associated with difficulty of voice use:

- Hard glottal attack (percussive sound to each word)
- Pressed phonation (perpetual overexertion of the respiratory system, squeezed throat, often initiated by a tight abdominal wall)
- Habitual muscle tension in the tongue, neck, and shoulders
- Poor breath flow
- Insufficient hydration
- Vocal abuse (habitual shouting, yelling, screeching, etc.)
- Habitual use of breath voice
- Inappropriate speaking voice pitch

Key Takeaways

- You have two voices: Inner and outer.
- Voice is movement, whether speaking or singing. Find freedom throughout the entire body to unlock its potential.
- Your voice is perfect; your use can be improved.

Activate—Activities That Allow You to Try It on

The Inner Voice

The Story of Your Voice

An informed approach starts with uncovering the layers that gave rise to our speech coordination. Much of what we say effortlessly rolls off the tongue, the timing between impulse and word choice being lightning fast. That was not always the case. Each of us learned to speak through an intense, effortful process that involved repetition, correction, and maybe even coercion. Around adolescence, speech patterns are redeveloped to maintain a connection with the herd. In developing a sense of self, young people begin to conscientiously experiment with language and vocality to fit in and set themselves apart.

Ask Yourself: What Is the Story of My Voice?

1 Who have I been told that my voice sounds like?
2 Where did I learn to speak?
3 Were you encouraged to use your voice as a child?
4 Were you forced or coerced to speak up or be quiet?
5 Were you ever punished for speaking up? How did you respond?
6 What feedback have you received about your voice? How did that make you feel?
7 When you listen to a recording of yourself speaking, what do you sound like?
8 Describe a situation where you felt at a loss for words.
9 How could you fill that space?
10 And what's next? Where do you need your voice to serve you in the short, middle, and long term?
11 What is the room or space where your voice will make the most impact, where it will enhance your life and the people's lives around you?

The answers to these questions form the story of your voice. It is an amalgam of thoughts, feelings, and information that informs the coordination that you utilize when speaking. Unconscious patterns can actively impede any process of change, so it is vital to do the excavating work of identifying where they are.

The Present Inner Voice

This exercise helps you to gain agency, directing the inner voice. Innocent mind wandering can lead to rumination. Sometimes, it is hard to feel that we can get our voice back on track to be a friend instead of a foe. Use the following steps to regain control.

1 Notice a negative running monologue of the inner voice.
2 Take a deep breath and exhale slowly.
3 Thank the mind for its wandering and visualize letting go of the last thought.
4 Do any somatic drill that re-regulates the nervous system.

   a Deep sigh
   b Yawn
   c Hum
   d Body tapping
   e Stretch

5 Assume you know nothing.
6 Direct your inner voice to make objective assessments about what is happening around you.
7 Only say what could be caught on a camera.
8 Only mention what is apparent right now.
9 Avoid predicting or recounting.

Reflection: After a few moments of directing the inner voice only to make objective observations, re-assess the state of your body and nervous system. What differences do you notice?

The Outer Voice

Children's Story

There is a natural storyteller inside all of us, but sometimes, it's hard to break out of our mold of speaking with monotone inflections and uninteresting cadences. The following exercise demonstrates how to combine your imagination and voice effortlessly with the skills you already possess:

1 Find your favorite children's book and read it out loud.
2 Notice the type of inflection, pacing, and volume you recruit when you are doing your most engaging storytelling.
3 Notice the sensations in the body that accompany communicating in this way.
4 Transfer those sensations to speaking about a more goal-related topic.
5 Titrate the excitement until it feels right for the room and the occasion.

Balance

We often carry unnecessary tensions in our bodies that prevent us from having optimal freedom in our movements. Return to the following exercise repeatedly throughout the day and before a demanding situation; it fine-tunes your proprioceptive sense of balance. This is the baseline for establishing ease and efficiency in voice use.

1 Stand/sit facing a mirror.
2 Allow your mind to quiet down.
3 Notice everything that your body is doing to keep you upright.
4 Ask yourself, can I do less?
5 Try on these words and move about the room with them in mind:

   a Buoyant
   b Springy
   c Bubbly

Reflection: Where did you find you could do less?

Breath

We often take our breath for granted because it is part of our autonomic nervous system. Nevertheless, focusing on the breath when searching for calm is highly effective because it is so "well-suited for relaying relaxation from the central nervous system (CNS) to the body and checking the arousal and homeostatic state of the viscera."[19] Try the following exercises at a calm, deliberate pace to cultivate a deeper sense of awareness of your breath.

1 Externalize the 3D breath.

   a Place your outstretched hands in front of you like you are holding the sides of a box close to your chest. Allow your hands to move laterally synchronized with the flaring of your lower ribs.
   b Place your hands one in front of the other. Synchronize with the movement of the belly and the back by increasing the space during inhalation and narrowing it during exhalation.
   c Stack your hands vertically with one hand close to the clavicle and the other close to the pelvic floor. Allow them to move further apart with each inhale and come closer together with each exhale.

2 Place one finger on a nostril to seal it while inhaling with the other nostril, and switch nostrils and fingers while exhaling. Repeat the process.

Develop Inclusive Awareness of the Vocal Tract

Sometimes we carry a level of tension in our muscles we are unaware of, even at rest. The vocal tract, which houses many different sets of muscles set at cross purposes is no exception. Before activating these structures, develop an awareness of their resting state.

With your body in balance and your mind at ease:

1 Notice the room, including its sounds, smells, sights, and sensations.
2 Notice how the body responds to weight and the force of gravity.
3 Notice how the breath moves the body.
4 Add awareness of the vocal tract physiology while at rest.

   a Is your larynx released?
   b Are your teeth clenched together or slightly apart? (A resting balanced position allows the jaw to fall away from the skull.)

5 Think about speaking. Which structures have an impulse to move?
6 Notice how the tongue responds.

   a Place a thumb under the chin and gently massage this area.
   b Is there a tendency to tense here when preparing to speak?
   c Can you still speak clearly with less tension here?

Semi-occluded Vocal Tract Exercises

Semi-occluded vocal tract exercises (SOVTs) are an evidence-based method of improving breath flow and vocal fold function.[20] These exercises encourage you to vocalize while introducing some momentary impediment to the vocal tract and then relieving it. This happens at such a fast rate that one hears a continuous sound, and the redirected airflow lengthens the vocal folds while activating the thoracic muscles responsible for regulating airflow. A quick online search will reveal a multitude of variations on this theme, along with visual demonstrations that you can imitate. A few that are accessible for beginners are included below:

1 Lip trills

   a Purse lips together to make a [p] sound
   b Blow until it starts to go on its own

2 Tongue trills [rrrr]
3 Raspberries
4 Humm [m] [n]
5 Continuants [v] [z]

Table 8.1 Primal sound exploration exercise

Yawn	Giggle	Cry	Hoot
Sigh	Laugh	Sob	Grunt
Hiss	Snort	Moan	Growl
Shh	Gasp	Groan	Fry

Primal Sounds

Table 8.1 lists primal sounds that can help activate a free and resonant voice. Find a space where you can make some noise, have fun with these sounds, and wholeheartedly explore your full range.

1 Explore these primal sounds.
2 Notice how the body engages to produce the sound.
3 Think of an important speech that you might give in the immediate future.
4 Practice initiating a primal sound and then merging it into your prepared material.
5 Playfully go back and forth between the two.
6 What do you notice?

Common Complaints about the Voice and Strategies to Address Them

Below is a simple chart that lists some of the most common vocal complaints and therapeutic strategies to remediate them.

Variety Act

When nervous, the variety in our vocal delivery is often the first thing to go. An easy way to find inspiration is to assess how entertainers who have a talent for evoking a response in their listeners use their voices.

1 Find a recording of a comedian you admire.
2 Close your eyes and turn up the volume.
3 Listen exclusively for their intonation.
4 Mimic some of the phrases and take note of the changes in pitch.
5 Now, make it relevant by practicing an upcoming speech with a similar delivery style.
6 Adjust the approach until it is suitable for the rooms you want to make an impression in.

Table 8.2 Voice troubleshooting guide

Issue	Root Cause	What Not to Do	What to Do[a]
Breathiness/ Softness	Vocal folds close too loosely, or space between arytenoids is left open (prevalent in adolescence). Inadequate adduction; excess throat tension	Recruiting neck muscles or use excessive tension. This can lead to injury	Say "uh oh" as if you've dropped a plate of spaghetti. Feel that gentle firmness of closure and extrapolate that coordination to other phrases you might use.[21]
Tightness/ Fatigue	Laryngeal muscles are overworking. Excess tension in the tongue, neck, and or pharynx (walls of the throat). Exclusive use of a small compass of the vocal range (limited inflection)	Pushing through and expecting it to resolve on its own or ignoring the feelings of fatigue.	Take a deep breath and sigh from the top of your range to the lowest note in vocal fry. Then invert the sigh from bottom to top. Babble like a baby on that easy air flow.
Nasality	Weakness or stiffness in the muscles that raise the soft palette.	Depress the tongue and larynx to try to get a lower sound.	Gargle with a liquid to activate sensation and motor activity in the palette and surrounding muscles. Use semi-occluded vocal exercises to jumpstart your phrase.

Note:
[a] This is not medical advice. Consult a speech therapist or medical professional if experiencing prolonged discomfort.

Vocal Hygiene

Lastly, here is some good old-fashioned advice for keeping your voice healthy. Do:

1 Hydrate
2 Rest
3 Get the blood flowing (cardio)
4 Warm-up (hum your favorite song)
5 Vocalize every day (Your muscles will atrophy, and your coordination will diminish if you are not actively engaged every day. Over time, this could lead to diminished capacity and ability.)

Don't

1 Speak in loud environments

   a Planes
   b Trains
   c Buses
   d Noisy restaurants

2 Smoke
3 Ignore acid reflux

Notes

1 Matthew Schloneger and Brian Manternach, "Technology Translated to Teaching: Exploring Vocal Dosimetry," *Journal of Singing* 76, no. 3 (2020), 321.
2 Molly N. Huston, Ira Puka and Matthew R. Naunheim, "Prevalence of Voice Disorders in the United States: A National Survey," *The Laryngoscope* 134, no. 1 (2024), 347–352. https://doi.org/10.1002/lary.30929
3 Molly N. Huston, Ira Puka and Matthew R. Naunheim, "Prevalence of Voice Disorders in the United States: A National Survey," *The Laryngoscope* 134, no. 1 (2024), 347–352. https://doi.org/10.1002/lary.30929
4 M. Perrone-Bertolotti et al., "What Is That Little Voice Inside My Head? Inner Speech Phenomenology, Its Role in Cognitive Performance, and Its Relation to Self-Monitoring," *Behavioural Brain Research* 261 (2014), 3. https://doi.org/10.1016/j.bbr.2013.12.034
5 M. Perrone-Bertolotti et al., "What Is That Little Voice Inside My Head? Inner Speech Phenomenology, Its Role in Cognitive Performance, and Its Relation to Self-Monitoring," *Behavioural Brain Research* 261 (2014), 220–239. https://doi.org/10.1016/j.bbr.2013.12.034
6 Nalini Ambady et al., "Surgeons' Tone of Voice: A Clue to Malpractice History," *Surgery* 132, no. 1 (2002), 5–9. https://doi.org/10.1067/msy.2002.124733
7 Nalini Ambady et al., "Surgeons' Tone of Voice: A Clue to Malpractice History," *Surgery* 132, no. 1 (2002), 5–9. https://doi.org/10.1067/msy.2002.124733
8 Davies, D. Garfield, Anthony F. Jahn, and Anat Keidar. "Development of the larynx and the voice." In Care of the Professional Voice: A Guide to Voice Management for Singers, Actors and Professional Voice Users, 12–16. New York: A Theatre Arts Book, 2004. Accessed September 12, 2025. http://dx.doi.org/10.5040/9781350054851.ch-002.
9 Dan Dediu, Rick Janssen and Scott R. Moisik, "Weak Biases Emerging from Vocal Tract Anatomy Shape the Repeated Transmission of Vowels," *Nature Human Behaviour* 3, no. 10 (2019), 1107. https://doi.org/10.1038/s41562-019-0663-x
10 Laura Allen and Amanda Hu, "Voice Disorders in the Workplace: A Scoping Review," *Journal of Voice* 38, no. 5 (2024), 1156. https://doi.org/10.1016/j.jvoice.2022.03.012
11 M. Perrone-Bertolotti et al., "What Is That Little Voice Inside My Head? Inner Speech Phenomenology, Its Role in Cognitive Performance, and Its Relation to Self-Monitoring," *Behavioural Brain Research* 261 (2014), 221. https://doi.org/10.1016/j.bbr.2013.12.034
12 W. S. Smith and Michael Chipman, *The Naked Voice : A Wholistic Approach to Singing* (Oxford: Oxford University Press, 2007), 17.

13 M. Perrone-Bertolotti et al., "What Is That Little Voice Inside My Head? Inner Speech Phenomenology, Its Role in Cognitive Performance, and Its Relation to Self-Monitoring," *Behavioural Brain Research* 261 (2014), 220–239. https://doi.org/10.1016/j.bbr.2013.12.034

14 M. Perrone-Bertolotti et al., "What Is That Little Voice Inside My Head? Inner Speech Phenomenology, Its Role in Cognitive Performance, and Its Relation to Self-Monitoring," *Behavioural Brain Research* 261 (2014), 220–239. https://doi.org/10.1016/j.bbr.2013.12.034

15 M. Perrone-Bertolotti et al., "What Is That Little Voice Inside My Head? Inner Speech Phenomenology, Its Role in Cognitive Performance, and Its Relation to Self-Monitoring," *Behavioural Brain Research* 261 (2014), 220–239. https://doi.org/10.1016/j.bbr.2013.12.034

16 M. Perrone-Bertolotti et al., "What Is That Little Voice Inside My Head? Inner Speech Phenomenology, Its Role in Cognitive Performance, and Its Relation to Self-Monitoring," *Behavioural Brain Research* 261 (2014), 220–239. https://doi.org/10.1016/j.bbr.2013.12.034

17 José Afonso et al., "Revisiting the 'Whys' and 'Hows' of the Warm-Up: Are We Asking the Right Questions?" *Sports Medicine (Auckland)* 54, no. 1 (2024), 23–30. https://doi.org/10.1007/s40279-023-01908-y

18 M. Latinus and P. Belin. "Human voice perception." *Current Biology*, 21 (2011): R143-R145. https://doi.org/10.1016/j.cub.2010.12.033.

19 Roderik J. S. Gerritsen and Guido P. H. Band, "Breath of Life: The Respiratory Vagal Stimulation Model of Contemplative Activity," *Frontiers in Human Neuroscience* 12 (2018): 397, https://doi.org/10.3389/fnhum.2018.00397.

20 Karin Titze Cox and Ingo R. Titze, *Voice Is Free After SOVT: Semi-Occluded Vocal Tract Principles, Methods, and Training* (National Center for Voice and Speech, 2023).

21 M. Perrone-Bertolotti et al., "What Is That Little Voice Inside My Head? Inner Speech Phenomenology, Its Role in Cognitive Performance, and Its Relation to Self-Monitoring," *Behavioural Brain Research* 261 (2014), 220–239. https://doi.org/10.1016/j.bbr.2013.12.034

Chapter 9

Communicating Like a Leader

Inform—Why It Matters

Warren Buffett, chairman and CEO of Berkshire Hathaway states that honing your communication skills can increase your net worth by 50%, adding that "A relatively modest improvement can make a major difference in your future earning power, as well as in many other aspects of your life."[1] Communication is a core competency for professional advancement, leadership effectiveness, and executive presence. It is a consistent factor in both initial interactions and evaluations over time.

Why communication matters:

- Executives – 85% say "clear and frequent communication from leadership" is the most critical factor in organizational resilience and employee trust.[2]
- Recruiters – 89% say bad hires typically lack soft skills, with communication cited as the most important.[3]
- Onsite workers – 43% lost trust in leadership due to poor communication.[4]

Communication is a key characteristic of executive presence, affecting initial interactions and evaluations over time. A leader who communicates well connects with others, inspires action, and enhances personal perceptions of competence and expertise.

Communicating well is not a skill that comes naturally. You may have taken a communication course in communication, but the motivation to pass the class is a world apart from the perspective you now have as a professional and leader. Today, your need to influence and engage with others productively allows you to understand the impact communication has on relationships and goal accomplishment.

In the 2019 book *Engineered to Speak*, top engineers and technical professionals from across the world were asked about the connection between

DOI: 10.4324/9781003624950-12

communication and professional advancement. Leaders from NASA, Deutsche Bank, Mercedes-Benz, and applied science industries recalled how their ability to communicate was a key factor in their advancement. It wasn't technical expertise alone that propelled them into top leadership positions, but an ability to communicate ideas in a clear and compelling manner to a variety of audiences.[5]

There are thousands of articles on leadership communication, but it boils down to three Cs of powerful communication:

1 Clear: Clearly communicate what you need from others, why it matters, and what you need them to *do* with the information.
2 Concise: You can lose someone's attention in less than six seconds! Conciseness is about getting to the heart of the message quickly and effectively.
3 Compelling: Why does it matter *now* and why does it matter to *them*? It's not about why the information is important to you. It's about the timely nature of the information and its potential impact on the receiver. Tell them why they should care.

Every communication interaction is an opportunity to influence. Whether by email, phone call, virtual meeting, one-on-one conversation, or larger meeting or presentation, the ability to articulate messages in a clear, convincing, and engaging manner is a hallmark of a leader with executive presence. At the end of this chapter, you will learn how to craft a leadership advocacy pitch. This tool prepares you to advocate for yourself by sharing stories of leadership experiences, achievements, and strengths. The challenge is to communicate a compelling narrative in one minute or less, putting the lessons of this chapter to use.

Equip—Skills or Behaviors That Enhance the Area in Focus

The goals of communication seem simple, but communication is complex because people's backgrounds, industry experience, subject matter expertise, motivations, and primed emotions vary.

Goals of Communication

There are three goals of communication:

1 Create shared meaning.
2 Express understanding.
3 Convey value and respect.

Creating shared meaning is dependent on message construction. You, as the writer or speaker, are attempting to convey a message that is easily understood by the receiver both in terms of content and intention. This has to do with word choice and message structure.

Barriers to creating shared meaning include differing levels of institutional knowledge, subject matter expertise, language or cultural differences, and emotional responses to the topic or sender. Creating shared meaning begins with understanding your audience and meeting them where they are.

The second goal is to express understanding, focusing on the meaning behind the message. First, we confirm the reception of the content, "What I hear you saying is that last week a team member dropped the ball and made it impossible to turn the project in on time." Then, we *express understanding* beyond the words, "It sounds like you are extremely frustrated!" Being able to paraphrase content, as you've understood it, allows the other to clarify if needed. Expressing what you perceive as the emotion behind the message allows for interpersonal alignment.

The third goal is to convey value and respect. If someone does not feel valued, they are not receptive to the message. This involves word choice, tone or voice, body language, respect for the other's time, and choice of delivery channel. When thinking about your choice of channel for delivery, should the message be an email or would it be better received as a call or face-to-face interaction? The context of the situation will determine the most appropriate channel for reception and desired outcome.

There are a variety of channel options. Face-to-face and virtual communication are the richest channels as they allow the most sensory input. We see one another, hear the various aspects of voice, read facial display or body language, while interacting in real-time to provide feedback or ask questions.

Phone calls are second richest channel. We rely heavily on cues taken from someone's tone of voice, volume, pitch, pace, vocal variety, pauses and even silence. Up to 90% of a message's meaning over the phone is taken from perceived auditory indicators.

Flatter channels include emails, texts, and letters. In fact, leaders should be highly aware of how they craft written messages. Think of a time when you opened an email and wondered about the tone in which it was written? Readers are prone to read *tone* and *intent* into an email or text based on a previous interaction with the sender or a pre-programmed response to the topic.

What do you do with an email, that if printed would be two pages long? How did opening that email make you feel? Did you read it immediately or close it thinking you might come back to it later? Did you feel your time was valued and respected by the individual that crafted the message?

Communication that conveys high levels of executive presence is strategic. It is clear and compelling and values the relationship and the other's time.

Richer channels, like face-to-face or phone calls, are best when trying to build relationships or where there is a potential for misunderstanding or conflict. Flatter channels like emails, text, and letters should be used for the simple transference of information. We can attempt to enrich written communication with an emoji to indicate emotion, but if you are concerned about how the message will be received, opt for richer channels.

If larger amounts of information need to be shared, consider reaching out with a phone call or quick meeting first to set the stage for why the information is important followed up by an email with the information that can be referred to in greater detail.

How can you create more effective messages and meaningful interactions? The key is to plan ahead. Before any important conversation or written communication, think strategically about three things: the communication opportunity, your audience, and your delivery method. This advance preparation positions you to be a more effective leader and communicator.

Three Strategies for Communicating with Influence

Leaders who communicate with presence know how to:

1   Analyze communication situations.
2   Lead with meaning.
3   Organize messages to increase receptiveness and retention.

Strategy 1: Communication Analysis

There are no perfect communicators, but preparation boosts your odds of success. The higher the stakes, the more preparation matters. Before you open an email or slide deck, begin to draft an agenda, or have a crucial conversation, ask yourself the journalistic questions of who, what, why, how, and when.

Ask the questions
The strategy is to jot down your answers to the following questions. This only takes a few moments but greatly increases the probability of message impact.

1   What is the purpose?
2   What is my desired outcome?
3   Who is my audience?
4   How is the information relevant to them?
5   What barriers may exist to creating shared meaning?
6   What is the best channel for delivery?

Think of an upcoming conversation, meeting, presentation, or written message you need to deliver. With this in mind, think through each of the following questions. In the Activate section, you will answer the questions more fully.

Q1 What is the purpose? To build rapport, to inform, or to persuade?

Q2 What is my desired outcome? At the end of this conversation/email/ presentation, what do I want my audience (one or many) to understand or be willing act upon? Be specific. Answer this in one sentence.

With the purpose and desired outcome in mind, you can drive the message toward goal achievement. To achieve my desired outcome, what information is most important to share? Think of this as reverse engineering.

Q3 Who is my audience?

Q4 How is the information *relevant* to them? Why should they care? What motivating factor would make them want to listen/read/learn/ act? How does it affect them (in accomplishing their job, personally, financially, etc.)?

It is imperative that you, either verbally or in written form, *state explicitly* the motivation of your audience. *What is in it for them, not you?* Recognize how the information affects your audience at a motivational or emotional level.

Q5 What barriers may exist to creating shared meaning? What is their level of knowledge and experience in terms of the topic? Are there objections that need to be addressed?

Q6 What channel is best for conveying information and ensuring understanding? Face-to-face, virtual, call, text, or email?

When deciding which channel is most appropriate for the interaction or message, choose between a richer or flatter form based on the communication context.

Should it be a phone call instead of a text or Teams message? A quick 15-minute Zoom with the entire team or a lengthy email? The higher the possibility of misunderstanding or conflict—the higher the stakes—the richer the channel should be. If reception of the message is crucial and time-sensitive, choose the most immediate channel that makes sense in the context of your organization's communication norms. Choose wisely.

Pro Tip: Confident communicators are agile. They analyze the situation, identify the purpose, and understand the audience prior to crafting their message. This strategic approach boosts clarity and connection.

Strategy 2: Lead with Meaning

Signal confidence through communication. Research published in 2022 by the startup artificial intelligence (AI) company Heyday found that "The average person consumes four articles, 8,200 words, and 226 messages daily." We are inundated with information! A confident communicator can cut through the noise.

To lead with meaning is to apply the journalistic method of opening with the most important information. Strategy 1: Asking the questions provides you with the ability to craft an open that secures your audience's attention. Securing their attention immediately indicates that you value their time and increases message reception. There are two simple steps to lead with meaning: (1) Craft a powerful open, and (2) state the *what* and *why*.

STEP 1: A POWERFUL OPEN

We are conditioned to engage in traditional "opens" like, "Hope you are well" or "Good morning, everyone. My name is Joe Smith, and I am here today to talk to you about ..." Break from the norm and create an open that commands attention.

In public speaking, this is called an attention-getting device. This can include a shocking fact, statistic, powerful quote, narrative, or question. Rather than, "OK, let's get the meeting started. Appreciate everyone for being here today." Start with, "Last month, our team's output fell by 15% costing the company $250,000." If you want to cut through the noise, open with a statement that will grab your listeners' or readers' attention.

STEP 2: WHAT AND WHY

Provide the meaning. Explicitly state the purpose, desired outcome, and why it matters to them. These statements are based on your responses to Q1 and Q2.

> Last month, our team's output fell 15%, costing the company $250,000. As our bonuses are tied to cumulative team output, the purpose of this meeting is to chart a clear path for success over the next quarter to make up for the loss.

Each time you begin to craft an email, plan a meeting, prepare a presentation, or plan for a one-on-one conversation of consequence, write out your opening statement. *This one simple strategy will elevate the perceptions of your leadership ability and executive presence.* People love a communicator who can get to the point and make the message matter!

Strategy 3: Organizing Your Message

You have a strong open, now organize the body of information so your readers or listeners can follow along. Don't fall into the trap of wanting to share *all* the information. Focus on the information that is *most relevant* to accomplishing your desired outcome. The most reliable approach is to follow the **Rule of Three**. Whether a lengthy email, meeting agenda, project update, one-on-one meeting, or formal presentation, if you break your talking points into three main ideas you increase perceptions of being a prepared and thoughtful communicator.

Break your information into three logical segments. Why three? Three is a memory device. Think of some popular slogans. *Snap, crackle, pop. Just do it. Life is good. I'm loving it.* Just like a slogan, if you break your information into three main parts, you increase audience receptiveness and information retention.

When Steve Jobs introduced the iPhone at the 2007 MacWorld Conference, he made the complex simple and the simple interesting. He focused on three aspects of the device, its inclusion of an: (1) iPod, (2) phone, and (3) internet search device. He followed the same process we are recommending. He had a strong open that secured his audience's attention, then introduced the topic (the revolutionary iPhone), by previewing three main aspects. This Rule of Three is especially important in public speaking.

Sylvia Ann Hewlett's *Harvard Business Review* article, "The New Rules of Executive Presence," cites a 2022 study showing 68% of respondents consider "superior speaking skills" as important to executive presence. In the Activate section, you will find a worksheet outlining a presentation or speech. This is a repeatable process.

Putting it all together, here is an example:

The open: Last month, our team's output fell by 15%, costing the company $250,000 and potentially impacting our end-of-year bonuses.

What and why: The purpose of this meeting is to chart a clear path for success over the next quarter. The goal is to make up for the loss and generate a win for the company and our team in Q2.

Organizational preview: We will examine three strategies for boosting: (1) Identifying current product-to-market fit, (2) generating fresh leads, and (3) expediting the client onboarding process.

Two of the most effective strategies for influential communication are leading with meaning and using a clear organizational pattern.

Making Meetings Matter

Whether you are in them or leading them, meetings can be a source of frustration. Many are a waste of our most valuable resource, time. If you lead meetings, whether in-person or virtually, return to the strategies: (1) Analyze the situation, (2) lead with meaning, and (3) organize the message. Leading a meeting is an opportunity to elevate others' perceptions of your leadership abilities. Leading an effective and efficient meeting takes planning, communication, and facilitated execution.

A meeting should have a purpose, agenda, and time frame:

- Purpose: You should be able to define the purpose of the meeting in one or two sentences at most. "This meeting is to plan the next phase of ..." or "The meeting is to make a decision regarding the new policy for handling ..." That way, everyone knows why they are there and what needs to be done.

   Tip: Include the purpose statement in your calendar/meeting invitation.
- Agenda: List the items you are going to review and discuss. Assign a time limit to each agenda item and identify the person responsible for speaking or sharing information. Try to adopt the Rule of Three if possible!

   Tip: Distribute an agenda in advance of the meeting to allow ample time for participants to prepare. Ask for input on the agenda from a few key members to socialize content and approach.
- Time frame: At the very least, set a start and end time. Also, set durations for each agenda item. These should total the overall meeting time frame – minus 10 minutes.

   Tip: This is where a facilitator is helpful, calling time on topic discussion and moving the group to the next item. It takes the pressure off you to manage the time.

There are some additional tips to help you successfully lead meetings:

Don't wait. Meetings need to start on time. Don't wait for the stragglers. When someone arrives late, don't go back and review what has already been covered. That just wastes the time of the people who showed up on time.

Remember, effective communication values others' time. Stay focused. Once you have communicated the purpose of the meeting and time allotment for each agenda item, you have permission to stick to it. A facilitator helps to keep control of time. If the group discussion becomes unfocused, don't be bashful. It never hurts to say, "Obviously there is more that needs to be discussed regarding this issue, but in the sake of time let's move to the next agenda item."

Create two roles for meeting management.

Role of the Meeting Organizer

- Determine participants and logistics.
- Define and distribute the agenda.
- Send out the meeting invite.
- Define and assign roles of facilitator.
- Outsource taking minutes to AI, whether virtually or in-person.
- Communicate any required preparation from the participants.

Role of the Meeting Facilitator

- Call time to progress through topics as determined by agenda.
- Ensure that everyone has a voice.
- If virtual, manage admitting attendees and responding to chat.
- Give the meeting organizer feedback after meeting.

Adopting new tactics for leading meetings with more efficiency is a great way to shift current perceptions about your leadership competency and elevate impressions of executive presence.

Leadership Advocacy Pitch

You are your best advocate! Increasing perceptions of executive presence requires you to become comfortable sharing narrative examples of your expertise and achievements. We often believe that our work speaks for itself. The truth is that if the work you are doing is going well, even accomplishing difficult tasks or lofty goals, it is not always recognized by those in power. It is not that they are trying *not to notice*, but that they are involved in their own day-to-day. This is a part of managing up. Equip others to tell the story of your work and advocate on your behalf. Making sure decision-makers are aware of your achievements, skills, and potential is crucial, since they can't advocate for what they don't know about.

Who are the people you should be telling your story to? What opportunities could you have to advocate for yourself? Maybe these are moments before a meeting when a leader asks you how things are going, a one-on-one weekly or monthly update meeting, or the classic elevator example where you are momentarily with someone you would like to impress. We do this through storytelling.

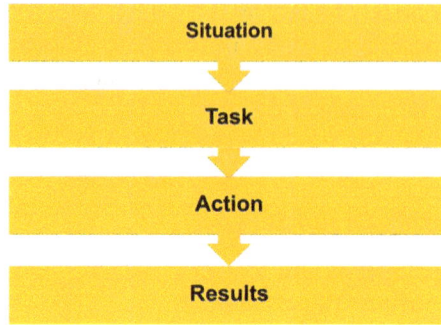

Figure 9.1 STAR method for leadership advocacy pitch

The STAR method provides a perfect framework for crafting a story highlighting an achievement. Using this framework, you can speak, briefly, about a situation, task assigned or self-assigned, actions taken, and results achieved. The goal is to create an encapsulated story that can be spoken in one minute or less.

Situation: Describe the situation that prompted the need for work to be done. "Last month, we were faced with a decrease in ... that caused..."

Task: What were you tasked with doing or what initiative did you undertake to solve the problem? "Our VP of Sales asked me to ..."

Action: What actions were involved in getting the work done? Things to consider: Talk about the role you played. What expertise of yours helped to facilitate the work? Don't be afraid to say "I" even when discussing team efforts. "I led the team in designing a plan that ..."

Results: What were the results and what impact did they have? Be specific and use measurements where possible. "These efforts increased our department's sales by 20%."

Use strategic adjectives when describing the work and your leadership. Think back to the three adjectives you chose in Chapter 1. Can you incorporate any of those "most desired" adjectives into the story? If one of your desired adjectives was "innovative" could you speak about your "innovative approach"?

In the following Activate section, you will be provided with a template to write out your leadership advocacy pitch.

Using AI in Crafting Communication

AI tools like ChatGPT, Claude, and Google Gemini excel as creative catalysts, helping you generate ideas, explore possibilities, and overcome the blank page. Beyond brainstorming, they serve as powerful writing partners – refining your prose, strengthening arguments, and clarifying complex concepts.

What makes these tools particularly valuable is their ability to accelerate your workflow: they can quickly synthesize information from vast datasets, draft templates for common communications, and provide multiple variations of your message. However, their true power emerges when you know how to direct them effectively.

The communication strategies outlined in this chapter will transform how you interact with AI tools. By learning to craft precise, strategic prompts, you'll generate responses that are not only well-organized but truly audience-focused. Instead of generic outputs, you'll produce communications that speak directly to your readers' needs, concerns, and decision-making processes.

Think of AI as your strategic communication partner—one that becomes exponentially more useful when you provide clear direction and context.

Take for example, developing an informative brief or project update. Designing a prompt based on the message's purpose, your desired outcome, audience, choice of channel, and time limit along with a prompt to outline information in three main points will result in a higher quality draft. You, then, become an editor adding, revising, and refining the presentation.

Professionals today use these tools as time-saving devices with great effectiveness. Whether in crafting emails, generating a meeting agenda, designing a performance plan, or presentation, clearly communicating what you need is the key. Erica Perl and Kenna Kay, who co-teach Written and Visual Communication in the Executive Education program at Johns Hopkins Carey School of Business, encourage their students to think of AI as an intern or assistant.

For research and writing tasks, Perl emphasizes that it's important to maintain a supervisory role. "Although AI gets more capable and sophisticated by the minute," Perl notes, "human intelligence is still necessary to verify, finesse, augment, adapt, and edit that which AI produces." Kay concurs, adding that AI tools can be useful for generating visual reference points, brainstorming, and explaining visual needs and preferences to professional designers. "You can also use AI for outlining and generating slides for a presentation deck," Kay suggests, "and then edit and add in your own content."

Activate—Try It on!

Communication Competence Self-Assessment

Let's begin the activation process with a self-evaluation of perceived communication strengths and weaknesses. Read through each statement relating to communication and assess your level of personal ability using the scale from 1 (none) to 7 (great) for each of the following statements as they apply to work-related interactions.

$$0----1----2----3----4----5----6----7$$

None-----------------Great

1 Feeling confident sharing ideas _____
2 Feeling comfortable with other's perceptions of you _____
3 Adapting to changing situations _____
4 Treating people as individuals _____
5 Being a good listener _____
6 Reasoning with people _____
7 Managing conflict _____
8 Generally knowing how others feel _____
9 Understanding nonverbal messages _____
10 Putting yourself in another's shoes _____
11 Being flexible _____
12 Using voice and body expressively _____
13 Asserting yourself (without becoming aggressive) _____
14 Expressing clearly what you need from others _____
15 Persuading people _____
16 Providing constructive feedback _____
17 Accepting feedback; being open to differing opinions _____
18 Letting others know you understand them _____

Reflection

Looking back over your Communication Assessment scores, choose one or two statements that you scored 5 or higher, considering them as strengths. Write about an example of each strength as illustrated in your interactions with others.

Choose one or two statements that you scored 4 or less on, considering them as areas of opportunity. Write about examples of perceived weakness as illustrated in your interactions with others.

Strategy 1: Answering the Questions

Think of an upcoming communication interaction or message you will be crafting. On a piece of paper, take three minutes to answer the following questions:

1 What is the purpose? To build relationships, to inform or persuade?
2 What is my desired outcome? At the end of this conversation/email/ presentation, what do I want the others to feel, remember or be willing to do? Be specific.

3 Who is receiving this message?

4 How is the information relevant to them? What's in it for them? Dig into the motivation of your audience to engage, understand the information, or be willing to buy-in or take action. What impact does it have on them (in accomplishing their job, personally, financially, etc.)?

5 What barriers may exist to communicating effectively? What is their level of knowledge and experience about the topic? Are there objections that need to be addressed?

6 What is the best channel for delivery? Face-to-face, virtual, phone, text, email?

Strategy 2: Lead with Meaning

Resist the urge to open with either of the following: "Hope all is well." "Thank you all for being here today. Let's get started." Use the same communication scenario from the previous activity. Craft an introduction that cuts through the noise.

The Open: Attention grabber

_____

What and Why: Purpose and why it matters to *them.*

_____

_____

Preview: Three main points to cover.

_____

_____

Strategy 3: Organizing Your Message

Follow these steps to organize your project update, brief, presentation, or speech.

1 Determine your purpose, desired outcome, audience motivation, and time allotment.

Purpose: _____

Desired outcome: _____

Audience motivation: _____

Time allocation: _____

2 Based on what you have determined is the most relevant information to help accomplish the desired outcome for this particular audience, break the information into three logical parts: Main Point 1, Main Point 2, and Main Point 3. This can follow a chronological order, categories of information, or even a problem, cause, solution if persuasive.

Body of presentation (three clear main points)

Main Point 1: _____

Main Point 2: _____

Main Point 3: _____

3 On a piece of paper or in a Word document, make three headings and then create bullets beneath each one to see what information belongs under each point. Examine the amount of information in terms of the time you will have to cover it and its relevance to accomplish your goal or purpose.

4 After you have organized the body of your presentation into three main points, it's time to take a creative approach and craft a powerful open— one that will capture your audience's attention and prime them for what you will be speaking about and its relevance to them. Following the "lead with meaning" principle, you should create a 30–90 second introduction using the elements below:

Elements of an introduction:

- Attention-getting device (a shocking fact, statistic, quote, or narrative)
- Link to topic
- Why now? Relevance (WIFT)
- Why you? Credibility statement
- Preview main points

> Attention-getting device: Studies on attention span indicate that you can lose someone's attention in less than eight seconds. The opening statement should be a moment that acts as an attention-getting device. Based on your topic, find a shocking fact or statistic, quote, creative statement, narrative example, or a rhetorical question.

> _____

> _____

> Link to topic: After the attention-getting device, a statement that links it to the topic at hand is needed.

> _____

> _____

Relevance to audience ("what's in it for them?"): A statement about why the topic is important to the audience. Why should they care about listening? What will they take away that is valuable for them?

_____

_____

Why you? Credibility statement

_____

_____

Preview of main points

_____

_____

5 Conclusion

- Restate purpose
- Review main points
- Strong close (return to attention-getting device)

Create a conclusion

Restate purpose:

_____

Review of main points:

_____

_____

Relevance (WIFT):

_____

Close (bring back to attention-getting device) or call to action:

_____

_____

6 **Leadership advocacy pitch**
    Recalling the three adjectives you would most like to convey, create a leadership self-advocacy pitch using the following framework:

Situation:

_____

_____

Task:

_____

_____

Action(s):

_____

_____

Result(s):

_____

_____

7 After you have written the pitch, say it aloud and edit for a more conversational tone. Do not try to memorize it. Do practice it enough so that you are ready with the story when the opportunity arises.

Practice makes better, not perfect

Communicating with a presence is about polish. In Carmine Gallo's 2014 book *Talk Like TED*, he stated that the top 50 TED speakers practiced an average of 200 times for their TED Talks. What does that tell us? No one is advocating that you practice a presentation 200 times, but run-throughs and constructive feedback help.

For the speaker, practice helps you to strengthen the quality and clarity of your information, and become comfortable hearing yourself; say it and physically perform it. Practice provides information about our use of time, language choice, body language, and voice.

Practice Step 1: Audio record

Record yourself on your phone delivering a verbal run-through. Recording the verbal portion of your run-through provides three important pieces of feedback: (1) The time it took from start to finish, (2) clarity of the information, and (3) the sound of your vocal delivery. Listen to the recording as objectively as possible and evaluate yourself using the measures below:

Time: _____

❑ Strong open/attention-getting device
❑ Stated purpose
❑ Motivated audience to listen
❑ Established credibility
❑ Previewed main points
❑ Logical sequence of main ideas
❑ Language is vivid, clear, fluid
❑ Voice is used effectively
❑ Conclusion is effective

Practice Step 2: Video record

On your phone or laptop, record a formal run-through. Watch your recording and provide a self-critique making additional changes in content or delivery. Check the time and adjust if necessary. Here is a self-critique checklist:

Content:

❑ How well did you gain your audience's attention?
❑ Did you have a clear preview statement/thesis?
❑ How did you reinforce your credibility?
❑ Was the presentation organized and easy to follow?
❑ Did you recap the most important information as you concluded?
❑ Did you end with a strong closing statement or call to action?

Delivery:

❑ What was the level of energy/dynamism?
❑ How did the gestures and nonverbal delivery enhance the presentation?
❑ How did you use your voice and inflection?

Practice Step 3: Peer presentation

Run through the presentation with a friend or colleague. Ask them to give you honest feedback about the information, its clarity, organization, and your overall delivery. Ask them to time you and to take notes as you present.

Time: _____

Introduction

❑ Gained attention and interest
❑ Stated purpose
❑ Motivated the audience to listen
❑ Previewed remainder of speech

Discussion

❑ Main points well organized
❑ Language: Vivid, clear, creative
❑ Identified with audience

Conclusion

❑ Summary clear
❑ Sense of closure

Delivery

❑ Level of animation/confidence/dynamism
❑ Gestures: Effective, appropriate
❑ Voice clarity, vocal emphasis

Notes

1 Catherine Clifford, "Warren Buffett Says This 1 Simple Habit Will Raise Your Worth by 50 Percent," *CNBC*, December 5, 2018, Englewood Cliffs, New Jersey. https://www.cnbc.com/2018/12/05/warren-buffett-how-to-increase-your-worth-by-50-percent.html
2 Deloitte Insights, *2023 Deloitte Global Human Capital Trends: New Fundamentals for a Boundaryless World* (New York, NY: Deloitte Development LLC, 2023). https://www2.deloitte.com/insights/us/en/focus/human-capital-trends/2023.html
3 LinkedIn Learning, *2020 Workplace Learning Report: The Rise and Responsibility of Learning and Development in the New World of Work* (Sunnyvale, CA: LinkedIn Corporation, 2020). https://learning.linkedin.com/resources/workplace-learning-report
4 Saisuman Revankar, "Communication Statistics," *ElectroIQ*, accessed May 27, 2025, https://electroiq.com/stats/communication-statistics/
5 Alexa S. Chilcutt and Adam J. Brooks. *Engineered to Speak: Helping You Create and Deliver Engaging Technical Presentations [electronic resource]* (Piscataway, NJ: Wiley-IEEE Press, n.d.).

Chapter 10

Building for What's Next

This final section provides opportunities for continued growth and development. A next-level step for many professionals is executive coaching. We have asked an expert to lay out the purpose and process of the coaching experience. Additionally, we have curated a list of podcasts, books, articles, and videos to provide you with avenues of further exploration along a variety of topics. Topics include executive presence, overcoming limiting beliefs, body language, voice, and performance psychology. These resources bring together expert perspectives and practical advice to advance personal insight, skills development, and to enhance overall confidence and executive presence.

Seeking an Executive Coach

An avenue for continued personal and professional development is executive coaching. As stated in Chapter 1, the need to cultivate executive presence is one of the predominant reasons leaders seek coaching.

Coaching generally involves three steps: (1) Finding the right coach, (2) clarifying your coaching goals (i.e. at the end of this three-month coaching engagement, I would like to have....), and (3) selecting a time period (six weeks, three months, six months) that meets your goals.

The International Coaching Federation (ICF) found that 53% of organizations report their senior leaders work with external coaches. The firm Upcoach.com cites that up to 60% of growth-stage CEOs surveyed used an executive coach. Leaders today, whether in corporate business, politics, or nonprofit, seek out coaching as a tool to navigate leading at the highest levels. Many companies choose to invest in coaching for their rising leaders because of the proven return on investment.

DOI: 10.4324/9781003624950-13

What Is Executive Coaching?

According to Dr. Carly Ackley, Director of Executive Education and Corporate Learning at Johns Hopkins Carey Business School, coaching provides transformative tools for leaders seeking to elevate their executive presence and maximize their impact. At its core, coaching is a structured, formal, and short-term process that is established to make progress and intentional change. When done well, coaching provides a space for leaders to reflect, action plan, and grow. Grounded in a professional relationship that is built on trust, coaching serves as both a mirror and a catalyst—providing space to explore one's personal leadership style while strengthening the confidence and composure that define executive presence.

Unlike consulting or mentoring, leadership coaching is a client-driven process. It's not advice giving. And it's not fixing other people's problems. Instead, a coach facilitates learning by engaging in active listening, asking powerful questions, providing growth focused feedback, and action-oriented dialogue, based on the developmental goals of the client. Through the coaching process, leaders are encouraged to identify their own agenda items, make intentional choices, commit to meaningful actions, and create accountability structures that cause behavioral changes and make habits sustainable for the long term.

The benefits of leadership coaching are felt at both the personal and organizational level. Leaders often experience stronger emotional intelligence, improved communication, greater resilience, and enhanced decision-making. They become more skilled at navigating ambiguity, building trust with others, and leading through influence rather than authority. These competencies are central to executive presence and in helping leaders project credibility, remain composed under pressure, and inspire confidence in others.

For those looking to deepen their leadership impact and continue to develop their executive presence through executive coaching, there are several avenues for finding credible coaches. The Office of Executive Education at Johns Hopkins Carey Business School offers the **Coaching for Leaders** program. This initiative connects professionals with experienced coaches to support their professional development in areas such as executive presence, strategic thinking, communication, managing career transitions, and leading high-performing teams. This offering is designed for leaders at all levels, and the program provides one-on-one coaching engagements that align with real-world leadership challenges and organizational goals. Whether leaders are navigating a transition, enhancing their presence, or leveling up their leadership style, *Coaching for Leaders* offers a personalized pathway to growth and sustained success. Learn more at: carey.jhu.edu/executive-education/coaching.

Additional Resources

Executive Presence

Podcasts

Speak Up: Develop Your Executive Presence and Leadership Communication Style

- Host: Laura Camacho
- Guest: Various guests focused on high-performing introverts and ambiverts
- Title: Episodes on executive presence in high-stakes meetings
- Links:

  - Apple Podcasts: https://podcasts.apple.com/us/podcast/speak-up-develop-your-executive-presence-leadership/id1368646965
  - Spotify: https://open.spotify.com/show/1KAGPr8yvRINtM6ZRZB0lv
  - Audible: https://www.audible.com/podcast/Speak-Up-with-Laura-Camacho/B0BJ6XX1HJ

Women at Work (Harvard Business Review)

- Host: Amy Bernstein
- Guest: Megan Bock (COO at Federato) and Laura Sicola (cognitive linguist and executive coach)
- Title: "The Essentials: Executive Presence"
- Links:

  - HBR Direct: https://hbr.org/podcast/2024/03/the-essentials-executive-presence
  - Apple Podcasts: https://podcasts.apple.com/us/podcast/women-at-work/id1336174427
  - Spotify

Men at Work Podcast

- Host: Travis Streb
- Guest: Business leaders and executives
- Title: "Embodied Leadership"—Episodes on integrating knowledge into experience and developing authentic leadership presence
- Link:

  - Apple Podcasts https://podcasts.apple.com/us/podcast/men-at-work-podcast/id1448969170

The Executive Leadership Podcast

- Host: Nathan Singh
- Guest: Alexa Chilcutt (Lead faculty of Business Communication for Executive Education at Johns Hopkins Carey Business School)
- Title: "Enhance Your Executive Presence"
- Links:

  - Apple Podcasts https://podcasts.apple.com/us/podcast/episode-43-alexa-chilcutt-enhance-your-executive-presence/id1665696754?i=1000662271892
  - Acast https://shows.acast.com/the-executive-leadership-podcast/episodes/episode-43-alexa-chilcutt-enhance-your-executive-presence

Books

Executive Presence 2.0: Leadership in an Age of Inclusion

- Author: Sylvia Ann Hewlett
- Summary: An updated exploration of executive presence that reflects how leadership expectations have changed due to the pandemic, political instability, and social movements. The book shows that while confidence and decisiveness remain paramount for gravitas, pedigree has become less central, with new emphasis on inclusiveness and respect for others. Found on Amazon. Link to book https://www.amazon.com/Executive-Presence-2-0-Leadership-Inclusion/dp/B0BZ94CYY4/ref=sr_1_1?crid=12R3FJY4KQBI7&dib=eyJ2IjoiMSJ9.1B6ooKytasrzB6WoKJNy3pz7DR7oHKl2JjMJMFqQHWXGjHj071QN20LucGBJIEps.eR-RTXYG-wNwWKU4wZT1Ell7ZM7cJhlU9qn-P-bz9WpE&dib_tag=se&keywords=Executive+Presence+2.0%3A+Leadership+in+an+Age+of+Inclusion&qid=1759880216&s=books&sprefix=executive+presence+2.0+leadership+in+an+age+of+inclusion%2Cstripbooks%2C71&sr=1-1.

Presence: Bringing Your Boldest Self to Your Biggest Challenges

- Author: Amy Cuddy
- Summary: Based on her famous TED talk, Cuddy explores how body language and personal presence can influence both how others see us and how we see ourselves. The book focuses on accessing personal power through presence, particularly in high-stakes situations, and includes research on power posing and confidence-building techniques. Found on Amazon.

- https://www.amazon.com/Presence-Amy-Cuddy-audiobook/dp/
B01944W6L8/ref=sr_1_1?crid=1M8EKCVYJGWUH&dib=eyJ2Ijoi-
MSJ9.2RQmIzd4D6Pv0FkEe-97t4ILQjCfefEhJ7PoRpaCwj8bG8HY
j75hgelCCn3ELEJsqQCZTRVhlY1ioU1mOHXEeTV4w6TC7lL61J-
8Rn95SYQ9C1j4Msxbd2nCvGamr_qYlZxsm6QB0Q-dsMGZk_
ejlF_9_0-2CenSl8IrSpSjE_-k.Q6fsmQy_sYmwP25RxBnt7VqDQgN
MNHmbMTXup50Nujs&dib_tag=se&keywords=Presence%3A+Bri
nging+Your+Boldest+Self+to+Your+Biggest+Challenges&qid=17577
98279&sprefix=presence+bringing+your+boldest+self+to+your+bigg
est+challenges%2Caps%2C99&sr=8-1

YouTube Videos

How to Develop Executive Presence

- Communication Coach Alexander Lyon interview with Allen Weiner, author, speaker, and executive coach.
- https://www.youtube.com/watch?v=Iy0i6mxF6vA

Executive Presence for Women Leaders

- Kevin Pho, MD interviewing cardiologist, Nandita C. Gupta. She shares her story and discusses her article, "Executive Presence for Women Leaders." https://youtu.be/QAuicpoAViU

Overcoming Limiting Beliefs

Podcasts

Leading and Living with Impact and Influence

- Host: Josh Kalinowski
- Guest: Various experts and successful professionals
- Title: Episodes on overcoming limiting beliefs and living a successful, fulfilling life
- Links:
  - Apple Podcasts: https://podcasts.apple.com/us/podcast/leading-living-with-impact-influence/id1469563081

The Mindset Mentor

- Host: Rob Dial
- Title: "The Skill of Self Confidence"

- Links:

  - Apple Podcasts: https://podcasts.apple.com/us/podcast/the-skill-of-self-confidence/id1033048640?i=1000706770866
  - Spotify: https://open.spotify.com/episode/3jtJJKEWOll2WaJ4JtwO6G?si=08671c7be9744cd0

The Impostor Syndrome Terminator®

- Host: Ines Padar
- Guest: Ambitious women entrepreneurs and business leaders
- Title: Episodes on overcoming subconscious success blocks and limiting beliefs
- Links:

  - Apple Podcasts: https://podcasts.apple.com/us/podcast/the-impostor-syndrome-terminator/id1559589441
  - Spotify: https://open.spotify.com/show/29IpVWSyfMM0mFz3gKdWsC

Impostrix Podcast

- Host: Whitney Knox Lee (Civil Rights Attorney and Racial Equity Consultant)
- Guest: Professionals of color in various industries
- Title: Episodes validating professionals navigating imposter syndrome and racial toxicity
- Links:

  - Apple Podcasts: https://podcasts.apple.com/us/podcast/impostrix-podcast/id1685421021
  - Spotify: https://open.spotify.com/show/5nZlSJI8eA0b0mB2JVD9lx

Trauma Rewired

- Host: Elisabeth Kristof, Founder of BrainBased.com
- Guest: Elise Besler, somatic voice coach
- Title: Empower Your Voice: Transforming Boundaries and Communication through Neurosomatic Intelligence
- Links:

  - Apple Podcasts: https://podcasts.apple.com/us/podcast/trauma-rewired/id1537602643?i=1000645101812

Books

The Secret Thoughts of Successful Women: Why Capable People Suffer from the Impostor Syndrome and How to Thrive in Spite of It

- Author: Valerie Young
- Summary: Written by an expert on the subject, this groundbreaking book addresses how imposter syndrome can strike anyone regardless of age, gender, profession, or racial demographic, and manifests differently in individuals based on personality traits and life experiences. Young provides practical strategies for recognizing and overcoming impostor feelings, particularly for high-achieving women in leadership roles. Found on Amazon. Link to book https://www.amazon.com/Secret-Thoughts-Successful-Women-Impostor/dp/B0CRZRLK16/ref=sr_1_1?crid=1EC2BNVAGRAON&dib=eyJ2IjoiMSJ9.YVgsAdayglwdFrGQZnMHBw.1TMtwqJ0YdyTgpNA1dOM_BQSNPcCJYHgMOdT9la8rk&dib_tag=se&keywords=The+Secret+Thoughts+of+Successful+Women%3A+Why+Capable+People+Suffer+from+the+Impostor+Syndrome+and+How+to+Thrive+in+Spite+of+It+%E2%80%A2+Author%3A+Valerie+Young&qid=1759880262&s=audible&sprefix=the+secret+thoughts+of+successful+women+why+capable+people+suffer+from+the+impostor+syndrome+and+how+to+thrive+in+spite+of+it+author+valerie+young%2Caudible%2C62&sr=1-1.

The Imposter Cure: Beat insecurities and gain self-belief

- Author: Dr. Jessamy Hibberd
- Summary: This book provides practical guidance on how to stop feeling like a fraud and escape the mental trap of imposter syndrome. Written by a clinical psychologist, it offers evidence-based techniques and exercises to help professionals overcome self-doubt and build authentic confidence in their abilities. Found on Amazon.
- https://www.amazon.com/Imposter-Cure-Beat-insecurities-self-belief-dp-1783256273/dp/1783256273/ref=dp_ob_title_bk

Own Your Greatness: Overcome Impostor Syndrome, Beat Self-Doubt, and Succeed in Life

- Authors: Lisa Orbé-Austin and Richard Orbé-Austin
- Summary: Written by psychologists and leadership consultants, this research-backed workbook helps readers understand and overcome imposter syndrome. The book provides practical tools and strategies specifically designed for professionals and leaders to build confidence

and authentic leadership presence. Found on Amazon. https://
www.amazon.com/Own-Your-Greatness-Overcome-Self-Doubt/dp/
B086WQKQ3F/ref=sr_1_1?crid=2EM91Q833XZPZ&dib=eyJ2Ijoi
MSJ9.LAv3Ezv5cGuLDQwyFaDjUg.wVU81pm7GWRu8tAwLLmvf
7TNkrkeaOowrV1Bl033zt8&dib_tag=se&keywords=Own+Your+G
reatness%3A+Overcome+Impostor+Syndrome%2C+Beat+Self-Dou
bt%2C+and+Succeed+in+Life&qid=1757798494&s=books&sprefi
x=own+your+greatness+overcome+impostor+syndrome%2C+beat+s
elf-doubt%2C+and+succeed+in+life%2Cstripbooks%2C95&sr=1-1

YouTube Videos

What Is Imposter Syndrome and How Can You Combat It?

Elizabeth Cox, TED-Ed
https://www.youtube.com/watch?v=ZQUxL4Jm1Lo

Carl Jung—Become a Luxury: How to Make Yourself Irresistible in Life and Business

Carl Jung Vision Channel
https://www.youtube.com/watch?v=nVhgWN_SuB4

The Power of Vulnerability

Brene Brown, TEDtalk
https://youtu.be/iCvmsMzlF7o?si=4YVCwET8ADrBJSrN

Body Language

Podcasts

The Art of Charm

- Host: The Art of Charm team
- Guest: Joe Navarro (Former FBI Special Agent)
- Title: "The Secrets of Body Language" | Joe Navarro
- Link: https://open.spotify.com/episode/33MUxSAI4PthYcyihrt09i

The School of Greatness

- Host: Lewis Howes
- Guest: Vanessa Van Edwards

- Title: "Why You're Lacking Charisma & How to Create It" Apple Podcasts Lewis Howes (Episode 1231)
- Link: https://podcasts.apple.com/us/podcast/why-youre-lacking-charisma-how-to-create-it-w-vanessa/id596047499?i=1000551736828

Books

What Every Body Is Saying: An Ex-FBI Agent's Guide to Speed-Reading People

- Author: Joe Navarro
- Summary: Joe Navarro, a former FBI counterintelligence officer and a recognized expert on nonverbal behavior, explains how to "speed-read" people: Decode sentiments and behaviors, avoid hidden pitfalls, and look for deceptive behaviors. You'll also learn how your body language can influence what your boss, family, friends, and strangers think of you. Found on Amazon. https://www.amazon.com/What-Every-Body-Saying-Speed-Reading/dp/0061438294/ref=tmm_pap_swatch_0?_encoding=UTF8&dib_tag=se&dib=eyJ2IjoiMSJ9.EIFvPZ9phrqPcjDUkQ90dpoKzg99v2Vl1MNbxDuCvGPzcJ35-iqT9Z0mlDhSMoIZ-SWbXNr0xrY2-dgqEwSX67dcY-7wKGc7JG-8s7aGRNQ6ws431dsNhbQTayrGRyTpZVnTN_OuB3ZjpRBpEmbltmvc-sxKHEF_3UksqbqRo6ZS-vuMYGfFYfMIJJnulmVh4.e_45g lPFRt87rJ2ZIsjgdQd1dFOi5JbUUPZkwEajvrM&qid=1757798572&sr=1-1-catcorr

Cues: Master the Secret Language of Charismatic Communication

- Author: Vanessa Van Edwards
- Summary: For anyone who wants to be heard at work, earn that overdue promotion, or win more clients, deals, and projects, the bestselling author of *Captivate*, Vanessa Van Edwards, shares her advanced guide to improving professional relationships through the power of cues. Found on Amazon. Link to book. https://www.amazon.com/What-Every-Body-Saying-Speed-Reading/dp/0061438294/ref=tmm_pap_swatch_0?_encoding=UTF8&dib_tag=se&dib=eyJ2IjoiMSJ9.EIFvPZ9phrqPcj DUkQ90dpoKzg99v2Vl1MNbxDuCvGPzcJ35-iqT9Z0mlDhSMoIZ-SWbXNr0xrY2-dgqEwSX67dcY-7wKGc7JG8s7aGRNQ6ws431ds NhbQTayrGRyTpZVnTN_OuB3ZjpRBpEmbltmvc-sxKHEF_3UksqbqRo6ZS-vuMYGfFYfMIJJnulmVh4.e_45glPFRt87rJ2ZIsjgdQ d1dFOi5JbUUPZkwEajvrM&qid=1757798572&sr=1-1-catcorr

YouTube Videos

Your Body Language May Shape Who You Are, **TED** Talk

- Amy Cuddy (Harvard professor and body language expert) https://www.youtube.com/watch?v=Ks-_Mh1QhMc&t=1s

Body Language Expert Explains How to Show Confidence | **WIRED**

- Joe Navarro (Former FBI agent and body language expert) https://www.youtube.com/watch?v=VRJzvJ5XPQI

Effective Communication Skills for Leaders

Podcasts

Speak with Presence

- Host: Jen Vellenga and Jennifer Rettele-Thomas (co-founders of Voice First World)
- Guest: Various communication and executive coaching experts
- Title: Interview episodes on leadership communication and executive presence
- Links:
  - Apple Podcasts: https://podcasts.apple.com/us/podcast/speak-with-presence/id1602443215

The Science of Succeeding

- Host: Brian Buffini
- Guest: Vanessa Van Edwards
- Title: "The Science of Succeeding with Vanessa Van Edwards"
- Link: https://podcasts.apple.com/us/podcast/s2e202-the-science-of-succeeding-with-vanessa-van-edwards/id1089027054?i=1000660145048

Think Fast Talk Smart: Smart

- Host: Matt Abrahams
- Link: https://podcasts.apple.com/us/podcast/think-fast-talk-smart-communication-techniques/id1494989268

Books

Lead Engaging Meetings: A Practical Guide to Maximize Participation and Effectiveness

- Author: Jeff Shannon
- Summary: *Lead Engaging Meetings* is the essential no-nonsense guide for professionals who want to transform their meetings into engaging, efficient, and result-driven events. Strategies within this book help you to transform boring, ineffective meetings into engaging, productive experiences—just by designing differently, changing your approach, and implementing the time-tested advice in this quick reference guide. Found on Amazon. https://www.amazon.com/Lead-Engaging-Meetings-Participation-Effectiveness/dp/B0CJXGKZ88/ref=sr_1_1?crid=1DD42NWUHDGET&dib=eyJ2IjoiMSJ9.ghu8jcmU9XjVKAV9eywT6YoEAPimBJ2Ihgtsvw0l3MA.BHHQr68bSqfTG-mB7CrAdFO1aGfd_2K3crU6hXxsBmY&dib_tag=se&keywords=Lead+Engaging+Meetings%3A+A+Practical+Guide+to+Maximize+Participation+and+Effectiveness&qid=1757798644&s=books&sprefix=lead+engaging+meetings+a+practical+guide+to+maximize+participation+and+effectiveness%2Cstripbooks%2C68&sr=1-1

Think Faster, Talk Smarter: How to Speak Successfully When You're Put on the Spot

- Author: Matt Abrahams (Stanford lecturer, podcast host, and communication expert)
- Summary: This book provides tangible, actionable skills to help even the most anxious of speakers succeed when speaking spontaneously. Abrahams provides science-based strategies for managing anxiety, responding to the mood of the room, and making content concise, relevant, compelling, and memorable. Found on Amazon. https://www.amazon.com/Think-Faster-Talk-Smarter-Successfully/dp/1035024977/ref=sr_1_1?crid=2O6H817KDMMW3&dib=eyJ2IjoiMSJ9.Xf2Y7yuYmko3EMzEsLCl7LpKCqKG_POsgCQP4oz-4vNxpwL8bH-G7vws-JJJ96v4pnQpmoxteyrbqEWdwujdYWTSfvm-LEPDYphPY2ii0xkeCX6N9EJYyPXtoLRldjxPdn.2h4rsTo60MxV2pcwRYAHWA7fE4hbHtmKtIGHD3eQZ1w&dib_tag=se&keywords=Think+Faster%2C+Talk+Smarter%3A+How+to+Speak+Successfully+When+You%E2%80%99re+Put+on+the+Spot&qid=1757798716&s=books&sprefix=think+faster%2C+talk+smarter+how+to+speak+successfully+when+you+re+put+on+the+spot%2Cstripbooks%2C65&sr=1-1

Never Split the Difference

- Author: Chris Voss (Former FBI hostage negotiator)
- Summary: Life is a series of negotiations, and negotiation is at the heart of collaboration—whether you are a business executive, a salesperson, a parent, a community leader, or a spouse. Chris Voss gives you the tools to be effective in any situation: Negotiating a business deal, buying (or selling) a car, negotiating a salary, acquiring a home, renegotiating rent, deliberating with your partner, or communicating with your children. Taking the power of persuasion, empathy, active listening, and intuition to the next level, *Never Split the Difference* gives you the competitive edge in any difficult conversation or challenging situation. This book is a masterclass in influencing others, no matter the circumstances. Found on Amazon. https://www.amazon.com/Never-Split-Difference-Negotiating-Depended-ebook/dp/B014DUR7L2/ref=sr_1_1?crid=99XSZX93LS2T&dib=eyJ2IjoiMSJ9.llOWRkk2tPaC1HWSFHKrm1KCQgYq137P-wjBMaeQ_eoPQwEPYLRV9yi-Kr7Qe6WGxKqH2pLafZC251p3MezLoP579l-5gn2F_oMw7i5RMb0-bxHexrWoQXpAWocMxRrp0eYn9xeFzOr-FUQunSuNR-PPci4V-dioFamOZYAEZSpKljMYZmZy1gy5WdlJR8u-Cuite3eEzrx6G4hpEcWRcqd9VTGhiL9au3qskIaGCYJP0U.6wsq89Oe CsEeLInffaPo4SC1XWmkpvIXdE91rbiKg7U&dib_tag=se&keywords=Never+Split+the+Difference&qid=1757798760&s=books&sprefix=never+split+the+difference%2Cstripbooks%2C81&sr=1-1

YouTube Videos

Communicate with Confidence: The Blueprint for Mastering Every Conversation

- Mel Robbins Podcast with trial lawyer Jefferson Fisher, communication expert https://www.youtube.com/watch?v=ZUCB3M_1Qp4

Improve Your Communication Skills with This! | John Maxwell

- John Maxwell Leadership https://www.youtube.com/watch?v=S0mbg U239ao

Voice

Books

The Human Voice: How This Extraordinary Instrument Reveals Essential Clues about Who We Are

Ann Karpf points out that we are overlooking one of the primary things people notice about us. The voice is more than a conduit for language:

The moment you open your mouth and start to speak, even if it's only to read from the phone book, your voice reveals, with remarkable accuracy, not only your sex, but your size, height, weight, and physique, and your health, education, mood, and social status. It tells your listener whether you are to be trusted, respected, or dismissed. And only the modulation of your voice makes you comprehensible at all: Transgress the normal codes of volume, pause, and pitch, and you can entirely sabotage conversations, turning sense into nonsense. Karpf's groundbreaking investigation uncovers the powerful messages that lie not just in what we say, but how we say it, and will make you hear the voices around you as if with new ears.

Found on Amazon.

Podcasts

Public Speaking with Peter George

- Host: Peter George
- Guest: John Henny
- Episode: Discover the Hidden Power of Your Speaking Voice with John Henny
- Link: https://podcasts.apple.com/us/podcast/public-speaking-with-peter-george/id1462669308?i=1000626478582

YouTube Videos

How to Succeed at Hard Conversations

- Host: Matthew Huberman
- Guest: Chris Voss
- Link: https://www.youtube.com/watch?v=q8CHXefn7B4

Vocal Branding: How Your Voice Shapes Your Communication Image

- Speaker: Wendy LeBorgne
- Link: https://youtu.be/p_ylzGfHKOs?si=AYxAKp99qRk-eVlv

Movie Accent Expert Breaks Down 32 Actors' Accents

- Erik Singer, Dialect Coach
- Link: https://youtu.be/NvDvESEXcgE?si=Tu-M99JDiyWvnaNX

Final Words of Inspiration

At the core of the Presence Principle is a call for a next-level challenge: How present are you willing to be?

Integrating executive presence into your interactions means continually assessing, adapting, acknowledging, and authenticating. This requires you to go past the safety of the comfort zone of habit and into the unknown growth zone of possibility. It can feel challenging to add these layers of consciousness to your day-to-day, but that is the key to creating that meaning, clarity, and flow.

Throughout the entire history of the universe there has never been another you. The millions, billions, and trillions of atoms around you may have met before, but your configuration is unique. Therefore, the strengths you possess cannot be prescribed or dictated, they must be mined and front of mind. That process and product are at the heart of the Presence Principle.

It is real work and it is iterative; you must go back to it every day. That is also what makes it inspirational. When others see you taking on this challenge and being responsive rather than reflexive, they can trust and rely on you when challenges occur. And they will!

We've noticed in our own lives and in those of our clients that challenging ourselves is a consistent state of being and looking to what's next. To integrate executive presence, you are meeting the best parts of you with the needs and desires of the moment. The opposite of embodying EP is to remain static, unaware, and uncurious.

Values, vision, and voice are the core components that enable us to engage in the Presence Principle.

In each situation, ask yourself:

- What are my values? Am I enacting them?
- What is my vision? Am I envisioning, then creating a strategy?
- What is my voice? Am I communicating my vision clearly? Am I using my voice to amplify my message?

And then, ask how do we measure it? How does one quantify or qualify progress?

- Values: A sense of ease
- Vision: A sense of clarity
- Voice: A sense of resonance

Return to the activities in this book again and again. Notice which ones get easier and which ones get harder. And by the way, make sure you are rewarding yourself on the journey. Simply continuing to take stock of things that might have flown under the radar for so long is an achievement. Bravo!

It takes courage and tenacity to remind yourself when you drift away from presence that it's time to come back. And yet, every artist, athlete, and intellect must continually activate this process. The ballet dancer returns to the barre, the pianist to the keyboard, and the painter to the canvas. The swimmer must go back to that pool every morning and the basketball player to the free throw line if they want to make sure their talent is there for them when they need it.

In our professional lives, we are the barre, the keyboard, and the canvas. We are the pool and the court. And we choose to begin each practice with curiosity. By continually asking yourself these questions, the answers you uncover will surprise you. They will connect you to your own *Presence Principle* and the unique ways that you can *embody executive presence and lead with impact.*

Index

Note: Page numbers in **bold** and *italics* refer to tables and figures, respectively.

3D breath, externalize 95–96
4-7-8 breathing 63

ability to engage 16
Abrahams, Matt 53, 128
Ackley, Carly 120
acknowledge, bias 39–40
adapt 40–41
affective stress management training 53
AI (artificial intelligence) in communication 110–111
AMP *see* anxiety management plan
anatomical points of balance 89, *90*
anxiety management plan (AMP) 53
anxiety-producing tasks 53
appearance 13–14, 17, 69
Ascough, James 54
assess, emotions 37–38
attentive ear gesture 77
auditory interpreters 12–13
authenticate 41
authenticity 8, 29, 41, 69; elements of 30; and values 29–30
authentic leaders 23, 30
autonomy **39**
avoidance 52

Baars, Richard 88
beauty **39**
behaviors 13–16
beliefs 51
Bernstein, Amy 121
Besler, Elise 124
bias 37
biofeedback hack 46–47

Bock, Megan 121
body 89
body language and virtual communication 15, 69–70; audit 82; behaviors 70–82; books 126–127; cultural considerations 81; facial display 72–73; frame for gestures 76–77; hand gestures 73–76; in meeting 82; in one-on-one conversation 82; podcasts 126–127; posture 70–71; power of silence 80–81; skills 70–82; speaking to group 82; virtually 82; virtual presence 78–79; walking with purpose 72; YouTube videos 128
body scan meditation 64
books: body language and virtual communication 127; executive presence (EP) 122–123; leadership communication 129–130; limiting beliefs, overcoming 125; voice 130–131
breath 89–91, 95
Brooks, Alison Wood 53
Brown, Brene 126
Buffett, Warren 101
Buffini, Brian 128

Camacho, Laura 121
ChatGPT 110
chest voice 91
Chilcutt, Alexa 122
Churchill, Winston 80–81
Clance, Pauline Rose 49
Claude 110

coaching 119–120
Coaching for Leaders program 120
code switching 41–45
code switch reframe **45**
coercive power use 23
cognitive biases 37
cognitive flexibility 41
comfort **39**; level of 69
communication: analysis 104–105;
    competence self-assessment
    111–118; convey value and respect
    103; creating shared meaning
    103; express understanding 103;
    goals 102–104; lead with meaning
    106–107; organizing your message
    107–108; powerful open 106;
    self-assessment 15; skills 15, 18;
    what and why 106–107; *see also*
    leadership communication
communicator 13
community **39**
competence **39**, 72
complete visualization 55
confidence 14–15, 17, 69; bias 40
confident but relaxed seated position
    71
confident communication 15
confident communicators 105
confident-yet-relaxed posture 70
consistent behavior 19
Contino, Richard 38–39
core values 33–34
Cox, Elizabeth 126
crying 88
Cuddy, Amy 70, 122–123, 128
*Cues: Master the Secret Language of
    Charismatic Communication* (Van
    Edwards) 127
cultural considerations 81;
    communication style 81; eye contact
    81; personal space 81
cultural norms 14

Desmet, Pieter 43
Dial, Rob 123
Donaldson, Steward 52
Dubin, Matthew 52

emails 103–104
Emerson, Ralph Waldo 23
emotion 69

emotional audit 45–46
emotional intelligence 19, 42–43
emotion intelligence and interpersonal
    integrity: behaviors 42–45; four As
    framework 37–42; overview 37;
    skills 42–45
emotion labelling 43
emotions 37; code switching 43;
    human needs, list of 43; label your
    emotions 43, **45**; naming 43
emotive visualization 56
enduring impressions 19; audit 24–25;
    behaviors 20–24; expertise 21;
    intellect 21; interpersonal integrity
    20; labeling your emotions **44**;
    negative presence 23–24; overview
    19; peak performance 22–23; skills
    20–24; values in action 20–21;
    vision 21–22
engagement 18; skills 69
Engineered to Speak 101–102
envisioning 22
EP *see* executive presence
execution of vision 22
executive coach 119
executive coaching 120
executive presence (EP) 24, 121;
    authenticity 8; behaviors 5;
    books 122–123; characteristics
    of 4–5; communication traits
    6; defined 3; gravitas traits 6;
    impression management 7–8;
    long-term impressions 6; overview
    3; podcasts 121–122; short-term
    impressions 5; skills 5; YouTube
    videos 123
*Executive Presence 2.0: Leadership in
    an Age of Inclusion* (Hewlett) 122
expertise 25
external message 50
eye contact 72–73

face-to-face communication 103
facial display 72–73
facial expressions 12
feelings: of fraudulence or inadequacy
    49; of self-doubt 49
Ferry, Korn 49
fitness **39**
flatter channels of communication
    103–104

flow, being in 52
Fokkinga, Steven 43
four As framework 38, 42; acknowledge 39–40; adapt 40–41; assess 37–39; authenticate 41–42
frame for gestures 76–77; seated in-person or virtual communication 77; standing in-person communication 76
"fresh eyes" perspective 16

George, Peter 131
Gerson, Richard 54
giggling 88
Glaser, Judith 40
Gleeson, Brent 21
goal-directed self-talk 55
goal setting 56–57
Goffman, Erving 7
Goffman's theory of impression management 8
good posture standing 71
Google Gemini 110
gravitas 14–15

habit 53
halo effect 13
hands: in "down" gesture 74; in "open" gesture 75; in "steeple" 75; in "stop" gesture 74
hands gesture box 76, 76; when seated 77
hands gestures 73–74; dos and don'ts 74–75, 76
Harris, Carla 8
head voice 91
Henny, John 131
Hewlett, Sylvia Ann 5, 29, 122
Heyday 106
Hibberd, Jessamy 125
high-quality virtual image 78
Holt, Penelope 38–39
Howes, Lewis 126–127
human attention 42
human imagination 84
human needs 39, 43
Human Voice: How This Extraordinary Instrument Reveals Essential Clues about Who We Are, The (Karpf) 130–131

imagery 55–57, 61
Imes, Suzanne Ament 49
impact 39
Imposter Cure: Beat insecurities and gain self-belief, The (Hibberd) 125
impostor syndrome/phenomenon 31, 49, 57, 72; beliefs 51; frequency, intensity, and disruptive impact of 51–52; in professional interaction 50; psychological skills of executive presence 52–53; signs of 49–50; sources of 50; transform 51–52
impression management 7–8; theory 7–8; as tool 8
impressive intellect 21
informed visualization 55–56
initial impressions: appearance 13–14; behaviors 13–16; communication skills 15; confidence/gravitas 14–15; overview 12–13; skills 13–16; social skills/ability to engage 16; status and reputation 13
inner voice 83, 86–88, 93; present 93–94
integrity 29
intellect 25
intelligence 72
internal thought or feeling 50
International Coaching Federation (ICF) 119
interpersonal dynamics 19
interpersonal engagement 69
interpersonal integrity 20, 25, 37
intersectionality theory 41
intoning 92
introduction framework 35, 35

Jung, Carl 126

Kalinowski, Josh 123
Karpf, Ann 130–131
Kay, Kenna 111
King, Martin Luther 81
"Know thyself" 29–30
Kristof, Elisabeth 124
Kumar, Subrat 69

larynx 84, 96
laughing 88

Lead Engaging Meetings: A Practical Guide to Maximize Participation and Effectiveness (Shannon) 129
leaders, follow the 45
leadership, role of 7
leadership advocacy pitch 15, 34, 109; STAR method 110, *110*
leadership communication: AI, use of 110–111; books 129–130; competence self-assessment 111–115; create a conclusion 115–118; goals 102–104; leadership advocacy pitch 109–110; meeting facilitator 109–111; meeting organizer 109; meetings 108–109; overview 101–102; podcasts 128; strategies for communicating with influence 104–108; three Cs of 102; YouTube videos 130
Lee, Whitney Knox 124
letters 103–104
limiting beliefs, overcoming: audit 57; behaviors 53–57; beliefs 51; books 125; concentration 57; deep flow audit 60–61; failure resume 59–60; goal setting 56–57; imagery 55–56; inner critic 49–50; mentor network 62–63; overview 49; podcasts 123–124; psychological skills of executive presence 52–53; real strengths audit 57–59; relaxation/regulation 53–54; self-talk 54–55; sharpen psychological skills 61–62; skills 53–57; somatic drills 63–64; trait *vs.* state 50; transform 51–52; YouTube videos 126
listening: deep listening 42; muscle 45; obstacle in 42; presence 43; to yourself 42
Little, Brian 51
Lyon, Alexander 123

Managing the Unexpected: Sustained Performance in a Complex World (Weick and Sutcliffe) 39
Maslow, Abraham 38
Maslow's Hierarchy of Needs 43, *44*
meeting facilitator 109
meeting organizer 109
megaphone *91*

mentor network 62–63
Merkel, Angela 81
mindfulness 54, 62
mindfulness behavior 51–52
Molinsky, Andy 41
morality **39**
moral leadership 37
multisensory visualization 55

narrative processing 46
Navarro, Joe 72, 80, 126–127
negative emotions 43
negative perceptions 13
negative presence 23–24
negative self-talk 50
Never Split the Difference (Voss) 130
"New Rules of Executive Presence, The" (Hewlett) 5
non-linguistic communication 84
nonobvious breakdown 39
nonverbal communication 69, 78, 80
nonverbal (body language) cues 14, 69

open-door policy 21
opportunity mindset 53
Orbé-Austin, Lisa 125
Orbé-Austin, Richard 125
organization's cultural norms 14
outer voice 83–84; balance 95; breadth 95; children's story 94; giving attention 85–86; *I don't talk at work* 86; primal sound improves efficiency 86–87; primal sounds 96–99; semi-occluded vocal tract exercises (SOVTs) 96; sound of my voice 85; strong, weak, nasal, or good voice 84–85
out of the box thinking 20
Own Your Greatness: Overcome Impostor Syndrome, Beat Self-Doubt, and Succeed in Life (Orbé-Austin and Orbé-Austin) 125–126

Padar, Ines 124
para-language 84
peak performance 22–23, 25
peak performers 22; traits of 23
Perl, Erica 111
personal introduction 35
person framed well within virtual "box" 79

Pho, Kevin 123
phone calls 103
podcasts: body language and virtual
    communication 126–127; executive
    presence (EP) 121–123; leadership
    communication 128; limiting
    beliefs, overcoming 123–124;
    voice 130–131
poor voice use 92
positive facial expressions 73
positive leadership 19
positive mental well-being 52
positive self-talk 72
posture 70–71
Powell, Colin 80
power of silence 80–81
*Presence: Bringing Your Boldest Self
    to Your Biggest Challenges* (Cuddy)
    122–123
*Presentation of Self in Everyday Life,
    The* (Goffman) 7
primal sounds 96–99; complaints
    about the voice and strategies
    97; exploration exercise 97;
    primer 88; variety act 97–98;
    vocal hygiene 98–99; voice and
    strategies 97
procrastination 52
professional introduction 34–35
progressive muscle relaxation 64
proof of credibility 13
protect/fear network 40
proxemics 78
psychological skills of executive
    presence 52–53
psychological skill training 57
purpose 39

Ray, Sundar 69
real strengths 57–59
recognition 39
reflection 22
regulation techniques 54
relatedness 39
relaxation/regulation 53–54, 57, 61
relaxation techniques 54
relaxed seated position 71
Rettele-Thomas, Jennifer 128
reward fulfillment 62
rise in testosterone 70
Romano, Melissa 54

sagittal plane of head 91
Schulte, Brigid 57
seated in-person communication 77
*Secret Thoughts of Successful Women:
    Why Capable People Suffer from
    the Impostor Syndrome and How
    to Thrive in Spite of It, The* (Young)
    125
security 39
self-awareness 37
self-confidence 69, 81
self-doubt 49–50
self-efficacy 41
self-questioning 49
self-regulate emotions 54
self-talk 54–55, 57, 61
self-touch gestures 73
semi-occluded vocal tract (SOVTs)
    exercises 96
sentiments of self-questioning 49
sequential visualization 55
Shannon, Jeff 129
silence 80–81; tips for using 80
Singh, Nathan 122
skills 13–16
SMART (specific, measurable,
    achievable, relevant, and
    timebound) goals 22, 56, 62
smiling 73
Smith, Ronald 54
snap judgments 12
social media 13
social skills 16, 18
somatic drills 63–64
sophistication 72
spaces, places, faces audit 46
sports psychology 53
standing in-person communication
    76
STAR (situation, task, action, result)
    34; for leadership advocacy pitch
    110, *110*
status and reputation 13, 17
steeple 75
stimulation 39
Streb, Travis 121
strengths-based attributes 31–32, 36
Sutcliffe, Kathleen 39

Teams 79
text 103–104

Think Faster, Talk Smarter: How to Speak Successfully When You're Put on the Spot (Abrahams) 129
Thirteen fundamental human needs 39
three Cs of of communication 102
time confetti 57
Todorov, Alexander 12
tone 84
trust building 42
trust network 40

value alignment and leading authentically: behaviors 31–35; core values 33–34; overview 29–30; professional introduction 34–35; skills 31–35; strengths-based attributes 31–32; value identification 32–33
value identification 32–33
values-based behaviors 19
values-based leader 29
values in action 20–21, 25
Van Edwards, Vanessa 126–127
variety act 97–98
Vellenga, Jen 128
verbal cues 14–15
virtual communication 77, 103; *see also* body language and virtual communication
virtual meeting 78
virtual presence 78–79; do's and don'ts 79; picture perfect 78; positioning 78–79; set the stage 78
vision 21–22, 25
visual and nonverbal behaviors 12
visual interpreters 12

visualization: complete 55; emotive 56; informed 55–56; multisensory 55; sequential 55; vivid 55
vivid visualization 55
vocal folds 83
vocal hygiene 98–99
vocal tract, awareness of 96
vocal variety 91–92
voice: books 130–131; podcasts 131; YouTube videos 131
voice-assistant technology 83
voice disorder 83
voice troubleshooting guide 98; breathiness/softness 98; nasality 98; tightness/fatigue 98
Voss, Chris 130

walking with purpose 72
warm-ups improve flow phonation 89
Weick, Karl E. 39
Weiner, Allen 123
What Every Body Is Saying: An Ex-FBI Agent's Guide to Speed-Reading People (Navarro) 127
Willis, Janine 12

Young, Valerie 125
YouTube videos: body language and virtual communication 128; executive presence (EP) 123; leadership communication 130; limiting beliefs, overcoming 126; voice 131

Zoom meetings 6, 79, 105

For Product Safety Concerns and Information please contact our EU
representative GPSR@taylorandfrancis.com
Taylor & Francis Verlag GmbH, Kaufingerstraße 24, 80331 München, Germany